RAISED BED GARDENING

A Beginner's Guide to Building and Sustaining Your Own Raised Bed Garden in Less Space

By Luke Smith

RAISED BED GARDENING

© Copyright 2020 - All rights reserved.

The content contained within this book may not be reproduced, duplicated or transmitted without direct written permission from the author or the publisher.

Under no circumstances will any blame or legal responsibility be held against the publisher, or author, for any damages, reparation, or monetary loss due to the information contained within this book. Either directly or indirectly.

Legal Notice:

This book is copyright protected. This book is only for personal use. You cannot amend, distribute, sell, use, quote or paraphrase any part, or the content within this book, without the consent of the author or publisher.

Disclaimer Notice:

Please note the information contained within this document is for educational and entertainment purposes only. All effort has been executed to present accurate, up to date, and reliable, complete information. No warranties of any kind are declared or implied. Readers acknowledge that the author is not engaging in the rendering of legal, financial, medical or professional advice. The content within this book has been derived from various sources. Please consult a licensed professional before attempting any techniques outlined in this book.

By reading this document, the reader agrees that under no circumstances is the author responsible for any losses, direct or indirect, which are incurred as a result of the use of information contained within this document, including, but not limited to, — errors, omissions, or inaccuracies.

RAISED BED GARDENING

Table of Contents

Introduction v

Chapter One - Why You Should Choose Raised Bed Gardening ... 1

Chapter Two - Deciding On Your Raised Bed Garden 17

Chapter Three - When And Where To Plant 39

Chapter Four - What To Plant In Your Raised Bed Garden 70

Chapter Five - Maintaining Your Raised Bed Garden 93

Chapter Six - Common Mistakes To Avoid 126

Final Words 142

INTRODUCTION

When it comes to growing plants indoors, the main approaches are either hydroponic (using nutrient filled water instead of soil) or container gardening. In contrast, the most common way to grow outdoors is to plant directly into the earth. But just because it is the most common doesn't mean it is the most appropriate. There are many reasons that you may not want to grow directly in the ground, one such reason might be that you have tested the soil and found it to be lacking. Or maybe you live in an area which is prone to flooding and you've learned the hard way that your garden is doomed to drown. The environmental factors make it so you need to grow indoors but maybe you don't have any space inside. When you find yourself in a pickle like this, what is a gardener to do?

One solution just might be to take the indoors approach to growing outdoors. Take those containers that would be used for houseplants and combine them with garden beds like you would find outdoors. Raised beds are essentially just large containers or tall garden beds. This approach to gardening may feel a little odd at first but there are many reasons that a gardener may want to explore the option. We'll take a look at these reasons in chapter one, but they are plentiful enough that raised bed gardening may be perfect for you even when environmental factors favor you.

Throughout this book you will learn everything you need to know to decide if raised bed gardening is the approach you should be taking when it comes time to plant your herbs, flowers, or vegetables. If raised bed gardening still intrigues you by the end of chapter one then the rest of the book will provide you with the knowledge necessary to build your own. Chapter two will look at how a raised bed garden is set up and how to choose the right size and material for your beds.

Chapter three continues this process by locking down the best time and place for your raised bed. Chapter four introduces us to the plants that grow best in a raised bed garden. We won't have enough time to get into every possible plant but those that are highlighted will be able to point you towards other possibilities and give you an idea of what attributes allow plants to grow well in raised beds and which make it difficult.

This will carry us naturally into chapter five to see exactly what work goes into maintaining a raised bed garden. Questions answered in this chapter range from how much water should a raised bed garden be fed to what is the best fertilizer and how often is it applied? Weeds, pests, and disease will each be addressed in this chapter as well. The book will then finish with chapter six and a look at some of the more commonly made mistakes that are easily avoided when you know what you are doing. By the end, you'll know not only if raised bed gardening is right for you but how to start your own and avoid the pitfalls that beginners keep tripping into.

It is my belief that you will come to find that raised bed gardening combines some of the best features of indoor gardening with those of outdoor gardening. It is this combination that makes this approach such a rewarding and refreshing avenue for starting your own garden.

CHAPTER ONE

WHY YOU SHOULD CHOOSE RAISED BED GARDENING

In this chapter we will explore the many benefits that come from growing your plants in a raised bed rather than in the ground. These range from considerations of the space they take up to the health of the plants, the effect it has on the human body, the way it affects the properties of the soil, and how it minimizes the amount of work needed to care for your plants. It is for these reasons (and more!) that people have begun to use raised beds more often in their gardens.

But before we even bother getting into the benefits, let us take a moment to define exactly what we mean when we use the phrase "raised bed gardening."

What is Raised Bed Gardening?

RAISED BED GARDENING

There is not one solid definition for the term. Different sizes, shapes, and designs that look entirely unique from each other can all fall into the category of raised bed. Rather, the term should be considered as a category under which many different approaches to gardening fit. Think of it almost like a movie genre. You have action movies but then under action movies are car flicks and martial arts films. They're all different but they share the same overall qualities.

We can extrapolate some information from the term itself. The fact that we are speaking about a raised bed means that we are planting our seeds above the ground level. How far above the ground level is up to the individual gardener. Your raised bed may only be raised up a couple feet off the ground but this isn't always the case. If you have ever seen a bed of flowers attached to a windowsill then you've seen another kind of raised bed. Windowsill beds tend to be at waist level (at the lowest) or chest level (at the higher end of the spectrum). So while the height varies quite a bit, the one definite thing that we can agree on is that the bed itself is above ground.

Another feature that is common among the various kinds of raised beds is the inclusion of a frame. Regardless of what the frame is made out of, its purpose is to separate the growing environment inside the bed from the natural environment around it. This frame is packed with nutritious soil and the walls of the frame prevents it from spilling out. Many gardeners choose locations that will allow them access to all four sides of their bed, however this isn't a feature of the raised bed itself but rather a product that arises from the gardener's design choices. Raised beds alongside windowsills don't offer this ability but that doesn't prevent them from being raised beds, after all.

While a frame is typical, they don't necessarily need to have a bottom. Many include a bottom to further separate the growing environment from the natural world but this feature isn't a given. However, a bottom will help to prevent pests from getting into your garden and we'll be treating the raised beds in this book as if they have a bottom.

So the prime characteristics that we use to identify and discuss raised bed gardens throughout the remainder of the book can be broken down into three features. These are beds that are above ground level, even if only one or two feet. They are designed to create a unique growing space which the gardener has total control of and which is separated from the natural world around it. Finally, these raised beds use a frame along the sides and the bottom in order to keep everything in place. When these three features are present, you have yourself a raised bed garden.

So now that we have this definition in hand, let us turn our attention to the question of why you would want to work with a raised bed in the first place.

The Benefits of Raised Bed Gardening

As mentioned at the start of this chapter, there are many different benefits that come from using a raised bed to grow your plants. These range from benefits that serve the plants to some which serve the environment, as well as benefits that directly affect the gardener themselves. You may not be interested in all of these but there are so many that you are certainly going to find yourself gravitating towards some of them.

Raised Beds Minimize the Space Needed to Grow: A raised bed functions much in the same way as a typical plant pot does. That is, it allows you to grow a plant in a space that is much smaller than is typically required when growing in nature. If you have a lot of room in your yard to grow plants, then this works really well when you are planting directly into the earth. But if you have limited space, then a raised bed may be just the thing you need to still be able to plant everything you want to. Raised beds allow gardeners to keep their plants in a single area and it removes the need to create rows such as typically seen when planting crops. Because you can fully circle around a raised bed, or at least don't need to walk through it at any point, you can grow a lot more plants in the same amount of space. Plus, a raised bed garden doesn't need to be on soil to begin with. Because a raised bed is filled with soil by the gardener, you could start a raised bed garden on top of a concrete parking lot without having any problems.

RAISED BED GARDENING

Raised Beds Look Amazing: While not a benefit in and of itself, this particular feature helps to accentuate the beauty of your garden. Since you can choose the material, shape, size, and design of the raised bed's frame, you have an almost limitless amount of possibilities when it comes to how your raised beds look. Many people go with wooden frames and don't pay much attention to them but others decorate their frames, choose materials such as hardened clay or concrete, and pair them with specific plants and flowers in order to bring out the beauty of the plants themselves. Others are less worried about how the frames pair with the plants but instead concern themselves with how the frames accentuate the overall impression of their landscaping.

Raised beds are thus able to serve as both a practical way to grow your plants and a way to decorate your yard.

You Don't Need to Bend as Much: While gardening is a favorite past time of many people across the globe, you will find that a lot of them agree that the worst part is all of the bending necessary to maintain the garden. You need to bend down to plant your seeds and carefully cover them with soil. Then, if you want to prune your plants, there's more bending to be had. You need to check for pests? That's more bending. You spotted a weed that needs to be pulled out? Best believe you're bending again. It's finally time to harvest? Even more bending. Those who are young and healthy might not give this a second thought but those older gardeners and those with bad backs certainly are used to the throbbing pain and sore muscles that this produces. One way to avoid this pain is raised bed gardening. While some raised beds are only a foot tall, there is nothing that says you can't build yours to be waist or chest level so that you can tend to your plants without bending over at all.

You Don't Need to Till a Raised Bed Garden: Another way that raised bed gardens save you from sore muscles is the complete lack of tilling necessary. When you grow in the ground, you need to till the soil between each crop that you plant. Tilling is the act of overturning, digging, or stirring the soil. This is done to help keep the soil nice and nutritious since the plants that were just harvested used their roots to suck up all the nutrients they could find in the soil. Large scale farming operations use specific machinery to till the soil but smaller gardens require manual work with shovels, rakes, and the like. Raised bed gardens don't need to be tilled between seasons. Instead, fertilizer, compost, or manure is added to the soil to provide it with the nutrients your plants need. Not only does this save you time and effort but the act of tilling soil can actually degrade the quality of the soil and so by cutting out the tilling process you are actually increasing the length of time your raised bed garden can go before needing to replace the soil with a fresh mixture.

Raised Bed Gardens Get Less Pests: In this particular case, pests refer not just to the annoying little insects that want to feed on your plants but also to larger animals like deer which can quickly destroy a garden if they aren't spotted immediately. Climbing critters like slugs and snails will be able to get into your garden but they are slow movers and if you are being mindful and keeping an eye on your garden then you should be able to knock them off before they are able to get into the bed itself. Since we are treating raised bed gardens in this book as having a bottom to the frame, annoyances like moles or groundhogs won't be able to get into the garden from the bottom. Deer can be tricky but some simple netting can be put up around the raised bed to prevent them from sticking their heads in. The biggest annoyances are going to be winged insects like whiteflies, some species of aphids, and male scales. It is pretty much impossible to block these tiny pests' access to your raised bed garden but some preventative measures such as neem oil applications will help to decrease the frequency of infestation and mindful maintenance will allow you to spot them early before they become a major pain.

Raised Beds Allows the Soil to Drain Better: As discussed previously, raised beds are an option to allow gardeners to grow in areas that deal with issues such as flooding. This is important to note because plants actually have a bit of an odd relationship with water. Water is one of the major resources that they need in order to properly grow and it is important to always provide your plants with plenty of the stuff. But too much of it can actually drown the roots of your plants and encourage them to start rotting. When root rot sets in, it can quickly spread to the stem and foliage of the plant and kill it in no time flat. Because of this, it is important to ensure that you use a decent draining soil to keep your plants healthy. But one way of altering the drainage speed of any soil is to elevate it up. The higher the elevation, the more room water has to seep out. Raising the level of soil is actually recommended for plants like succulents when they are grown in the earth but by raising our garden beds we create this same effect and it helps us to keep our plants free of rot without taking any extra measures.

RAISED BED GARDENING

Raised Beds Get Far Less Weeds: Harking back to the point about tilling the soil, we left out one of the negative effects that tilling produces. When you till soil, you are moving it all about and mixing it up and one of the effects this has is to distribute seeds throughout the soil that will in time grow into weeds and start trying to spread. The lack of tilling leads to a lack of weeds. However, this doesn't prevent weeds in general and there are many ways which they might get into your raised beds. One trick to handle them that gardeners use is to cover the top layer of the soil with something like plastic or cardboard. This is done at the start of spring in order to suffocate and kill off anything that took root throughout the winter. Without access to sunlight, water, or oxygen, these winter intruders quickly die off.

Simply remove the material you added, pull out the dead weeds, and your raised bed garden is ready to plant. Other weeds may get into a raised bed garden by growing up underneath it but if your frame has a bottom then you won't need to deal with this. You may still find the occasional weed in your raised bed garden but it will be a rarity rather than a regular occurance.

By Controlling the Soil, You Avoid Contamination: One of the problems with modern day gardening is the fact that we have done a lot of damage to the soil around us. Runoff from chemical plants or chemically treated crops can degrade the soil quality of the areas around it and cities are prone to allowing heavy metals like lead into the soil due to all the technology and metal that they are filled with. This is a problem because vegetables you grow for human consumption can ingest these metals and cause sickness both in the plants and in us humans. This is one of the reasons that plants in urban areas are typically moved away from the road or have hedges around them to create a barrier. But the single best way to avoid contamination through soil is to use a raised bed for your gardening needs. You add the soil to the raised bed and can ensure it is of the highest quality and clean of any contaminants. This allows you to rest easy knowing that your plants are as healthy as possible and you aren't going to get sick if you eat them. After all, isn't the whole point of growing veggies to eat healthy?

Other Benefits: Two quick benefits before we move onto the next chapter. The first is that you don't need to commit to using a raised bed every year. You can build and start using a raised bed one year, decide it isn't for you, and break it down the next. Or, you can set your bed in one spot, realize that it isn't the most effective use of the space, and then move the bed before the next spring. This offers a level of flexibility that you can't get when growing in the ground.

Also of note is the fact that using a raised bed garden will allow you to plant your seeds earlier in the year compared to a traditional garden. This is an amazing benefit that we'll discuss more in chapter three.

RAISED BED GARDENING

Chapter Summary

- There is no one concrete definition of what constitutes a raised bed garden. In order to give a better sense of what we mean, we look for the presence of three key features.

- The first feature is the fact that the garden bed is raised. This could be a foot off the ground or it could be as high up as you want, the key element is that it is above ground level.

- The second feature is the inclusion of a frame. A raised bed garden may only have four walls around it but throughout this book we are going to treat our raised beds as if the frame also provided a bottom for further protection.

- The final feature is the fact that a raised bed garden is a self-contained growing space that is separate from the natural world. A raised bed needs to be placed in a frame and filled with soil and whatever grows inside of it is kept apart from the earth beneath it.

- There are many benefits to starting a raised bed garden which make them an excellent choice. What follows are some but far from all of the benefits provided by raising your garden bed.

RAISED BED GARDENING

- Raised garden beds allow gardeners to fit more plants into a smaller area, thus making it a perfect fit for those with limited space.

- Raised beds sit above ground level and use their own soil, which means that you can tend a raised bed garden on a paved surface.

- Raised beds add a charm to any yard and the varied colors and designs make them a beautiful addition to any landscaping project.

- Because of their elevated height, raised garden beds are fantastic for those with bad backs. Since there isn't as much bending involved, your muscles don't end up sore.

- Tilling the soil is necessary in most garden beds between seasons but this degrades the overall quality of the soil. Raised garden beds use fertilizer and compost to enrich the soil to keep it effective for longer.

- Due to their height, it is much harder for pests to get into a raised garden bed. Critters like deer are still a problem but can easily be prevented through the addition of a simple net fence.

- The elevated height of a raised garden bed increases the drainage speed of the soil and makes it easier to avoid harmful problems like root rot which are caused by overwatering.

- Tilling the soil helps to redistribute weed seeds throughout the soil. Raised garden beds avoid this by skipping the tilling process and any weeds that have taken root can be killed off at the start of spring for easy planting.

- While most prevalent in cities, even the soil in the countryside may be contaminated with chemicals or heavy metals like lead. This is a problem when planting in the ground but a raised garden bed is its own growing environment and is thus free from contamination.

- A raised garden bed can be removed at any time. If you want to change it up between seasons, this is easy to do. If your plants get sick and pass then you can remove the raised garden bed even during the growing season.

- Raised garden beds also let you plant your seeds earlier in the year, which is great for growing big, bountiful crops of delicious vegetables.

In the next chapter you will learn how to go about setting up your own raised bed garden. This includes determining the best material for the bed to be made out of, whether or not it is better to go small or big, what choices you have in terms of the design of the bed, and everything else you need to get started with the bed itself.

CHAPTER TWO

DECIDING ON YOUR RAISED BED GARDEN

Now that you have chosen to start your own raised bed garden, you must be pretty excited to get started. Unfortunately, getting started first means planning and deciding on the specifications of the raised beds themselves. So it isn't time to get your hands dirty quite yet but that doesn't mean you can't have a ton of fun with this process.

You are going to need to decide on some very important features that could entirely change the way that your raised bed garden looks, feels, and functions. These features include the size of the beds you will be raising up. There is no single right answer for what size they should be; that is entirely up to you. But it is important to be aware of how size changes the function of the garden. Likewise, you are going to need to decide on what type of material to use for the bed's frame.

Again, this is your choice and so we'll be looking at all sorts of different materials to see the pros and cons of each. Finally, it is also important to choose a design. A raised garden bed doesn't just need to be a rectangle. You'll discover tons of raised bed garden designs that you can copy or use to brainstorm your own. When it comes to this step, your imagination is the limit and that's what makes it so much fun.

Big Garden Bed or Small Garden Bed: Which is Better?

When it comes to size, we need to consider width and height primarily. Length is going to be determined by how much space is available in the garden. You could have a raised garden bed that goes on forever (if you had the space). This infinite bed could produce quite well as long as it had enough height for the roots of the plants and small enough width for you to be able to check and tend to each plant. Length doesn't need to factor into considerations of size and so we can toss any concerns about that particular variable out the window.

Left with width and height, we can start to address the question of whether it is better to be big or small. The answer to that actually a little complicated in that the best answer is "either." The real problem in size doesn't come from being big or being small but from being too big or too small. With size, the problem areas are on either end of the size chart (tiny or huge) but the middle section of that chart (small or big) is a perfect fit for your raised garden bed. Let's start with width.

If your raised garden bed isn't wide enough then you may not have any space to grow your plants. It is easy to look at a garden bed with a tiny width and know that your plants won't fit and so this isn't a problem that most gardeners run into. The more common issue is to have too wide of a raised garden bed. This is the gardening equivalent of the old adage, "eyes bigger than your stomach." While the equation "more room = more plants" is technically true, what this leaves out is the fact that you are still required to tend to those plants. If there is too much space for you to reach over, then you aren't going to be able to get at the plants in the middle of a wide raised bed. This leads to mistreated plants and signs of sickness or infestation going unnoticed until it is too late. So how do we go about making sure that our raised beds aren't too wide?

The best rule of thumb is to make them no wider than four feet across if you have access to each of the sides. If you have a garden bed with a side that you can't get to, because it up against your house for example, then you should knock a foot off that. If you go over this size, you may not have problems getting to the plants in the middle while everything is still just a seedling. But once their foliage really starts to come in and the bed fills out, suddenly is it much harder to get to those tricky-to-reach plants. Keep in mind, this number is an average based on the height and reach of most people. If you are shorter then you should knock half an foot off your width. Taller gardeners can get away with adding a little to the width but this could be an issue if you need to go away and get someone to watch over your garden.

Height is an easier calculation to make. The average height for a raised bed is between half a foot to three feet tall. However, as we are primarily discussing beds with a bottom, we should stick to at least a foot in height. The taller a bed is, the more soil you have added to it. The roots of your plants are going to spread out in that soil and search for nutrients. A smaller bed in the half a foot range would need to use a mesh bottom in order to prevent critters from accessing your garden from below while also providing the roots access to the natural soil beneath. A small raised bed of this height is going to contradict some of the benefits that we discussed in the previous chapter such as reducing pests or weeds and avoiding contaminated soil. So what we need is a bed high enough that the roots don't run out of space. That's a foot at the minimum. If you are planting lots in the raised bed then you may want to go even taller.

Going taller is going to have a few different effects. One, it is going to allow for better drainage in the bed. But it is also going to trap moisture for longer. So the water will drain away from the roots quicker but there is much more soil to drain through and so the bed will hold the moisture longer. This means that the taller a bed is, the less it is going to need to be watered. This is doubly good because most raised garden beds use wooden frames and the more they are exposed to water, the quicker they will decay and need to be replaced.

Speaking of the wooden frame, it is important to remember that the soil inside the frame will be pushing it outwards. That is, the soil doesn't just want to stay in place but rather gravity is always pulling at it to spill everything. Because of this, the soil in the bed puts pressure on the frame. The taller the bed is, the more pressure there is. A weaker wood might work fine for a foot tall garden bed but the pressure of a three foot tall bed may shatter the wood and spill all over your yard. The taller the bed is, the thicker the wood that needs to be used. Other materials like concrete can also be used but these will present their own problems.

So the secret to a perfectly sized raised garden bed is to keep it at least a foot tall and no more than four feet wide. Beyond that, you are free to do as you want. Just remember that more soil equals more pressure on the frame. Speaking of frames…

What's the Best Material for Your Raised Garden Bed's Frame

When it comes to the material you make your frame out of, you have a ton of choices. You can use everything from cement to pallets, railroad ties, or even tires. There is an abundance of choices so long as you can provide four walls (or three, even as low as two depending on the features of your space). For instance, stack four tires on top of each other and place them on a piece of wood, fill it with dirt, and you've got yourself a raised garden bed. A little creativity can give you some really amazing options.

But a lot of the time these materials can actually prove to be bad choices or even harmful ones. That tire garden we just created? Might look really great but tires are known to carry heavy metals that can poison the soil. The benefit of avoiding contaminated soil goes right out the window when you use tires. Of course, this doesn't mean you shouldn't always use them. If you are planning to grow flowers or succulents, something you aren't planning on consuming, then tires could still be a good fit. That's just one example, let's dive into the rest.

Stone: Stone can be a beautiful material to build a raised garden bed out of. It is expensive as can be from the store but if you can find it locally or have some on your property then you could use this. You will need to purchase mortar to fill in the gaps, keep it all together, and block weeds' entry to the bed. These beds can cost a lot of money to make but once they are built they can last forever. We still have stone walls from ancient history all over the world. This makes the money worth it but consider it carefully because removing it will be a lot of work.

RAISED BED GARDENING

Brick: Brick walls are another option that lasts forever and also uses mortar so it makes sense to cover them together. Brick walls are pretty much like stone walls except that where stone walls accentuate the natural aesthetics of a yard, brick walls disrupt it. This can fit perfectly into many different styles of raised garden beds and landscaping designs but that is the primary difference between the two. Though brick can often be more expensive than stone, so people will purchase old concrete blocks and treat them as if they were bricks.

Railroad Ties: Railroad ties are a popular choice for a recycled material that creates a feeling of American heritage, like something right out of a Norman Rockwell painting. They look absolutely great in a garden. But unfortunately they're also a harmful choice that should be avoided at all costs. Railroad ties are treated with more chemicals than you could imagine and a whole whack of them makes you sick. Worse than heavy metals, these ruin the soil around them and so they shouldn't even be used for flower beds. They're a thousand times worse than tires and the EPA has even warned about the dangers of gardeners using them.

Shipping Pallets: You find shipping pallets used in a lot of raised gardens because they are a cheap material to purchase second hand. However, you don't know what they were used to transport and pallets more than fifteen years old may have been treated with harmful chemicals. If you can find out what they were used for and when they were made then shipping pallets may still be a good fit, but if you can't find out this information then it is best to avoid them rather than risk both the health of the soil around them as well as your own.

Cedar: Cedar, as well as redwood, is a strong wood that lasts a long time. They don't rot very quickly, they don't hold in a lot of moisture and they aren't even appealing to most pests. They look quite striking and accentuate the natural elements of a yard but since they are wood they do rot. You can expect a good half decade out of them but they will need to be replaced over time.

Treated Lumber vs Untreated Wood: Treated lumber is pretty great if you are building furniture. They have been treated to rot slower and be less appealing to pests and so they make a smart choice if you need to build a bookshelf. But a garden? You're going to want to stick to untreated wood since those same chemicals which boost the treated stuff are going to poison your soil. Untreated wood is going to look gorgeous and accentuate natural elements but they're going to rot much quicker. Cedar is an example of an untreated wood (pretty much the best untreated wood) but pretty much anything works. The only real problem is how quickly the wood you pick starts to rot. Rot is going to determine the speed at which you need to replace pieces of your frame.

Choosing the Design of Your First Raised Garden Bed

You've already seen how much freedom of choice you have in the size and material that you can make your raised garden out of. Both of these, together, pale in comparison to the options you have for designs. If you can think of a way to provide four walls to keep all your soil in place then you can pretty much make any raised garden bed you want. If you're really creative you can get away with three walls in a triangle design. There really is a limitless possibility here when you add a little bit of creativity. With that said, let's look at a bunch of different designs to get our imaginations working.

Rectangle Beds: The most common style is the simplest. Take two pieces of wood the same size for the length, two pieces the same size for the width, and stick it all together. These are best used for vegetables or herbs rather than flowers because aesthetically they look the most like a classic vegetable patch you'd see in a yard.

RAISED BED GARDENING

Spiral Bed: This bed is easiest done with brick or stone because it needs to have a natural curve to it that can be difficult to achieve with wood. Starting at the base, build a spiral out of rocks that slowly gets taller and taller towards the center. This design is beautiful with flowers or even herbs and the really cool thing about it is that it allows you to grow a lot more plants in the same amount of space when compared to the earth.

Windowsill Beds: A windowsill bed can be a great way to grow herbs or small vegetables if you live in an apartment or if you live in a house then a small windowsill bed can let you maximize your available space to grow as much as possible. Stick a small, foot deep rectangular garden bed to your window so that all you need to do to tend to it is open the window. A clever use of this design is to stick one to the window in your kitchen and grow fresh herbs you can grab when needed.

Multi-Level Beds: One of the coolest approaches and best ways to maximize your available space is to create a multi-level bed with two, three, four, or even five levels depending on what you can reach. Each level is going to need to be roughly a foot deep but you can grow all sorts of different plants on each level. In as little as four by four feet you can grow an entire garden salad with a raised bed in this design.

Border Beds: Made out of whatever you want, one of the most common ways you see raised garden beds being used is to create a border along paths or driveways. By building up a garden bed, you can line a pathway to make it clear which way traffic (on foot or on wheels) is supposed to flow. Rather than sticking up a sign, this approach creates a natural and beautiful pathway that is easy to follow.

Bench Beds: Gardens are beautiful to look at and there are a thousand romantic movies involving meaningful kisses on park benches. You can make it easy to soak in the beauty of your raised garden bed by building benches into the side of the frame. As long as the material you use is strong enough to support the pressure from the soil and the weight of a human then this approach can create a beautiful place to sit in your garden and enjoy it. Not only is this aesthetically pleasing but it can offer a place to sit while you tend to the plants or harvest the veggies or at the very least it offers a surface to place your tools on.

"Coffee Table" Beds: A coffee table sits on four legs and you place stuff in the middle. A "coffee table" garden bed sits on four legs but the middle grows plants instead. Four legs lift up a middle section at least a foot deep that hangs in the air. This design is a beautiful addition to areas with benches, picnic tables, or other sitting areas in which one might have a hot dog or a beer out back.

Tire Beds: We already talked about these but they make an easy way to add some circular imagery into your yard and so long as you aren't growing edible plants then they won't cause you any harm. If you are purely looking towards tires to add circular imagery then one available option is to create the raised garden bed you want with tires but then build up stone or brick around it and yank the tires out. This will give you more natural circles, and less harmful ones at that.

Choosing the Right Soil

In chapter five we will be discussing how to maintain the health of your raised garden bed soil but the first step in keeping it healthy is to start with a proper soil. There is no such thing as a perfect soil but there are quite a few options available for healthy, long-lasting soils. This in and of itself could be said to describe gardening as a whole. No matter how much you do right, there is always a little bit of room for random chance to throw you a curveball. But by using a great soil, you minimize the chances of that curveball catching you by surprise and taking out your garden bed before you realize it's too late.

One of the reasons that soil is so important for this stems from the fact that overwatering plants can cause them to rot and lead to diseases. Raised garden beds help to limit this chance by giving plenty of room for water to drain out. But in order for water to drain at all, you need to be using a soil that has plenty of space between the substances it is made from. You will also need to consider the pH level of the soil, which is another feature that we will be talking about more in chapter five. For the time being, make sure that you find out the pH level required by any of the plants you are planning to grow in your raised garden bed. We'll be looking at plenty of wonderful options for what to grow in chapter four.

RAISED BED GARDENING

We want to make sure that our raised garden bed has a soil that is rich in nutrients. While we will be adding nutrients to the bed through the use of fertilizer later on, we must create a mixture that has plenty of nutrients to begin with so that our plants can absolutely thrive in the soil. We get these nutrients by mixing compost into our soil. While dead plant matter in your garden is something you are going to want to remove, you can purchase (or make) a compost mixture which is healthy for your plants. While it is often made out of similar plant matter that had once been alive, it is important to note that the compost we use with soil has been treated to kill off harmful pathogens. The plant matter that falls off what you're growing is untreated and diseases and pests fester and multiply there.

RAISED BED GARDENING

The best soil for a raised garden bed is a 33-33-33 mixture made up of compost, vermiculite, and either peat moss or coconut coir. The compost is going to provide the nutrients while the vermiculite and the peat moss work together to alternatively trap water and let it drain quickly. If you were too lean on just one then it would drain too quickly for the plants to drink but if you let it absorb too much without draining then the plants would rot and drown. It is important to note that plants don't just absorb nutrients from the soil on their own. They need water, a macronutrient itself, to wash over the nutrients so that the roots can drink them up.

While you can and should get your vermiculite, peat moss, or coconut coir from your local garden center, you are actually better off making your own compost. If you are looking to just get started then a bag of compost isn't going to hurt you but there will be many more nutrients in a homemade mixture. A great compost for raised bed gardens mixes in cut grass, kitchen scraps such as fruit or vegetable peelings, egg shells, or shredded cardboard. Manure is also a nutrient rich substance which mixes well in a compost. You should avoid meat and whole fruits or vegetables. It is better to go with scraps here. In order to make sure that you have a range of nutrients, you should always have a minimum of five different items in your compost. This helps to even out the nutrient ratio and provide a ton of micronutrients as well.

You should keep in mind that you may need to alter the soil you use depending on what you are looking to grow. Say you are looking to grow succulents rather than vegetables. In that case you would want a soil that is even more loose and you may even want to skip the compost all together to focus on a more sandy or rocky soil. The three part mixture we've made in this chapter is a great fit for most garden vegetables and many flowers but adding a few minor changes to it will allow it to fit more specific uses. In chapter five we'll talk about when and how we amend the soil to keep it rich and healthy. But first, let's turn our attention to where and when we plant our raised bed gardens.

RAISED BED GARDENING

Chapter Summary

- Before you can start growing anything in a raised garden bed, you must first *have* the raised garden bed and this takes a little bit of planning. The size of the bed, materials of the frame, and shape of the design are all going to change the feeling of your bed.

- You can have a garden bed of any length you want but the width should be no more than four feet or the space furthest you can reach and properly tend to a plant.

- The height of your raised garden bed should be at least a foot since we are using bottoms to protect our plants.

- A raised garden could be as small as half an foot but then it would need to use a net bottom to allow the plant's roots enough space to grow.

- The taller a raised garden bed is, the more pressure is going to be pushing against the frame. Taller beds will require frames made from stronger materials.

- Tires make for an interesting looking garden bed but they should only be used for flowers and other plants you aren't planning on eating.

RAISED BED GARDENING

- Stone is a strong material which can withstand a lot of pressure and will last pretty much forever. Mortar will need to be used to keep it together and the raw materials are quite expensive.

- Brick also uses mortar and is expensive. Some people use cement bricks to cut down the cost but either material breaks the natural aesthetic.

- Railroad ties look rustic in a garden but they're so deadly you should never use them for anything and the EPA has put out warnings about them.

- Shipping pallets may be cheap but you must be able to find out their history before you use them.

- Cedar is a strong, untreated wood which will last five to ten years and look gorgeous as part of a raised garden bed. Other untreated woods are also good choices but they'll rot at different rates.

- Treated lumber lasts longer but that's because of chemical processes that will poison the soil and so it is best to avoid any type of wood that has been treated.

- The easiest raised garden bed design is a rectangle or square bed but there are many

RAISED BED GARDENING

designs ranging from spirals to multi-level beds that ascend like staircases.

- When it comes to picking the right design for your raised garden bed, you should let your creativity run. There are almost limitless options when you truly let yourself have fun.

- The best soil you can pick is one that holds onto water long enough for the roots of your plant to suck up nutrients while also draining fast enough to avoid drowning and causing the roots to rot.

- Compost is a great way to mix nutrients into your raised garden bed soil but not all compost is made the same. Dead plant matter that falls off the plants in your garden needs to be removed to limit the risk of infestation or infection.

- The best mixture for a raised bed garden is an even 33-33-33 spread made of one part compost, one part vermiculite, and one part either peat moss or coconut coir. This soil will be great for most North American garden vegetables but it should be tweaked based on the needs of the plants you are going to be growing.

- Making your own compost will result in a more nutrient rich mixture. Vegetable peelings, shredded cardboard, and cut grass are all great additions to a compost mixture. Avoid adding meat or milk products. For the richest compost possible use at least five different ingredients.

In the next chapter you will learn when and where it is best to start your raised bed garden. The when refers to the season of the year and the weather necessary for your raised bed garden to thrive. The where discusses the physical location of your raised bed garden and how to determine what location is the best. Ultimately, the location will be determined by the needs of the plants you decide to grow but knowing what you can grow requires you to understand each possible location you have identified as a space for your raised beds.

CHAPTER THREE

WHEN AND WHERE TO PLANT

Both when and where are necessary questions to ask before you plant anything. You should always make sure that you know the environmental conditions you are planting in and how they are expected to change throughout the coming season. It will be stressed in the coming sections but you should get used to checking the weather every day to see if there is anything you have to worry about. Always make sure to look at the forecast for the following week when you check, making note when storms or heat waves are predicted.

While functioning much the same as any garden bed, a raised garden bed gives a slight advantage to gardeners looking to get a head start on their crops. You can typically plant a raised garden bed earlier than one in the ground. However, you are going to need to be careful and take what you are growing into account. Not everything should be started at the same time, after all.

In this chapter we will start with the question of when. We'll see what season is the best for planting a raised garden bed and we'll take into consideration all of the elements we should be looking out for to tell that the time is right. Following the when, we'll look into the mystery of where. You can place a raised garden bed pretty much anywhere you want if you're creative but you are going to find yourself in a bit of a pickle if you don't consider what you are planning to grow during this step. Finally, we'll add in a little how by seeding our first raised garden bed.

When to Plant a Raised Bed Garden

Again, the primary factor in when to plant is going to be determined by what you are planting. Tomatoes are going to need warmer weather than lettuce, for example. When looking up information about the crop you are planning to grow, don't just look up the ideal temperature. If you are asking for help at your local garden center then remember to ask at what temperature will seeds fail to germinate and what are the extremes (both hot and cold) that the plant can withstand. Lettuce will grow under 40F but tomatoes will die before their vines even start to come in.

Most garden plants go in the ground during the spring. Those that can withstand lower temperatures go in early spring, those that need warmer temperatures go in late spring. This means that most plants are ready to harvest in the summer, though some can be harvested throughout the entire summer while others benefit from extra growing time before they harvest. If you are looking to grow harvestable plants then you are going to need to pay attention to two key details both when planting and when harvesting.

First, you need to be mindful of when the last frost of the winter season is. Typically, you don't plant anything before this date. If you start your plants inside with the intention of transplanting the seedlings to an outside raised garden bed then you will plant seeds roughly three weeks before the last frost is scheduled but when planting seeds directly into the bed it must be after this. Similarly, if you are growing harvestable fruits, vegetables, or herbs then you are going to need to keep track of when the first frost of the winter season is. Many harvestable plants can't survive a frost and so they will need to be done harvesting before this time. However, there are exceptions to this rule such as parsnips which taste better after a frost or two. Individual plants have a tendency to break all the "rules" of gardening but they are the exceptions.

The other element you need to pay attention to is the temperature of the soil. Plants are going to want to have a soil temperature that is somewhere between 60F and 70F. This isn't true for all, as there are plenty that can withstand lower temperatures and their seeds will even germinate better at a lower temperature, but for the most part you are going to need 60F if you want seeds to germinate properly. Get yourself a soil thermometer and check the soil temperature daily. If you are also paying attention to the weather every day then together these two habits will help you to figure out what weather factors affect the soil temperature and in time you will be able to judge simply by checking the weather channel. Keep in mind though, even gardeners who have acquired this skill take a reading of the soil before planting. It always pays to be safe and use accurate data when deciding if it is time to plant or not.

Furthermore, whether you are planting seeds or transplanting seedlings, you shouldn't plant a raised bed garden when the weather is overly windy or it is raining. Rain is a problem for many reasons, not the least of which is the health of your plants. You want the soil to be dry when planting and then to water it afterwards. Wind is bad because it can blow away seeds, though careful sowing can take care of this. Seedlings, on the other hand, are easily damaged and stressed out by the wind. If you haven't hardened off your seedlings prior to planting them the wind is pretty much guaranteed to kill them.

Finally, we've so far addressed when to plant as if it only happens once a season. True, if you are growing tomatoes, peppers, or eggplants, any of those crops that take a long time to mature, then you are going to be planting once a season. But if you are growing something like lettuce then you could be harvesting and planting several times a season. Lettuce and spinach are two plants which you can harvest early and still enjoy as microgreens. Depending on how large you are looking to grow the crop, you could actually plant them up to three times starting from the last frost and harvesting just prior to the first of the new winter.

RAISED BED GARDENING

Where to Set Up a Raised Bed Garden

You have two choices when it comes to where to set up your raised bed garden. The first is to set it up anywhere you want, making sure it is aesthetically pleasing to accentuate the natural beauty of the yard. The other choice, the one we will be focusing on, is to carefully plan out where you are going to set up your raised bed gardens so that you can grow exactly what you want with the highest chance of success. First, however, let's talk about the limitations of aesthetic beds.

When you set up a raised garden bed in a spot without first considering the environmental conditions of that space, you limit what you are able to grow there. Typically, when you are picturing the garden bed itself, you likely have an idea of what would fit. Aesthetic beds are mostly used for flowers rather than harvestable crops like fruit but even so you have probably already envisioned what color the flowers that fill the bed will be. If this is true then you should stop, research the needs of those flowers, and then build the bed. To assume that they'll work fine can lead to big disappointment and beds that don't have the same eye-popping beauty that was intended. When you just place beds without thinking about what is going to go into them, you limit your choices for what you can grow there.

But planning doesn't have this same limitation. When you plan out what you want to grow (which we'll be looking at in the next chapter) before you set up your bed, you can make sure you place it in the perfect space to provide as much sun, shade, and wind protection that that species requires to thrive. This level of understanding and control over the space you build your raised bed garden in will allow you to take precise control over your garden through careful consideration and monitoring over the course of a few days. Simply put, planning your space carefully is what separates beginners from experts and there's no better way to start your first garden than doing it like a pro.

If you know what you want to grow, then you should research their temperature and sun needs and write it down. There are going to be a few factors which determine if a spot is right for a raised bed garden or not; how much sun and shade, the temperature of the spot, the drainage quality of the spot, how much wind protection it has, and how well the spot can be protected from critters. This doesn't even take into account the aesthetic appeal of the spot. However, this doesn't mean the aesthetic appeal of a spot isn't worth consideration but rather that it is an extra consideration to put on top of these and one that relies on personal taste to decide. But for now, you may want to jot down each of these elements on a piece of paper and use this as your guide to picking a spot.

The first element on that list is how much sun or shade the spot you are considering gets. Some plants, tomatoes for example, love to get tons of sun. They want to have any and all shade held back so that they can turn a beautiful red. Thankfully, it's not sunburn but a sign that they're ready to be harvested and enjoyed. But tomatoes are just one example. There are plenty of other plants that don't need nearly that much sun and instead prefer to grow in the shade. Lettuce is one such example. Lettuce likes to get some sun but too much can send it to seed and ruin your plans for next week's salad.

To figure out how much sun or shade a location is getting, watch it throughout the course of a day. Set a reminder to glance over at the spot once every hour or two and watch how much sun it gets throughout the day. Be mindful to watch in the afternoon in particular as shade may come and go depending on what is casting it. Doing this will let you know exactly how much sun a spot can provide. Whether a spot is shaded or not doesn't make it better or worse. It just changes what plants can grow there. But by knowing this, you don't make the mistake of trying to grow something that will only suffer in the space.

While you are checking the sun throughout the day, it can be a good idea to go out into the space and take a temperature reading. Stick the soil thermometer in the ground and see how hot the soil is when the sun is on the spot. Do the same reading when it is shaded. Get one last reading just before bed. This will give you some fantastic data. You can see the difference between a shaded space and full sun space to get a sense of the range of temperatures that your plants will be dealing with. Of course, these temperatures will rise as the weather warms up but the range between them in the shade and in the sun will stay roughly the same so you can use this to predict the behavior of the weather and each plant's tolerance for what the space offers. Places with more shade will have lower temperatures but this can help you to grow a range of plants if you can place one raised garden bed in the shade and another in full sun.

Next to consider is drainage. Now, the drainage quality of your raised garden bed is going to be strongly determined by what soil you use and we covered this in the last chapter. But there are a few factors of the physical space that will affect drainage. Smaller raised garden beds are going to have bigger issues being placed at the bottom of an incline. If you are building your raised bed frame to have a proper floor then it is important not to forget holes for drainage. These should be drilled straight through the wood and then covered with a mesh to prevent large pests from getting in through the bottom. If you forget this step then drainage is going to be a huge issue. Consider how much shade or sun the spot has, as well. More sun will result in quicker drainage while shady spots hold onto moisture in the soil much longer. Being aware of all the factors that contribute to the draining speed of your soil will help you to never overwater and drown your plants by accident or lack of knowledge.

RAISED BED GARDENING

Wind protection is not always an important factor but it can be depending on the species you are looking to grow. Delicate plants do well to be kept out of the wind, especially if your local climate is a stormy one. Wind protection can come from a building, such as a window ledge bed would have. You could also add protection in the form of netting, boxes, or carts. When used creatively, you can add wind protection to a garden bed while also adding to the beauty of the yard as a whole. Raised garden beds are simply one of the most gorgeous features a property can have when they are full of wonderful and healthy plants. But they're not so pretty when they are full of broken, beaten, and wind-struck plants. Noting the level of wind protection a bed has will allow you to avoid this unfortunate experience. It always pays to be prepared.

Finally, consider how well protected your raised garden beds will be from critters. A lower bed is more likely to be attacked by pests like slugs, snails, aphids, or whiteflies, but not so much a taller bed. Beds without solid bottoms are at a higher risk of being attacked by burrowing critters, though a solid bottom will typically prevent this. If you don't add netting over the draining holes of the flooring then you may have a burrowing creature to deal with but otherwise you should be fine. Meanwhile, really high up beds still need to be concerned with mice, deer, squirrels, and other animals. While these may prove to never be an issue, it isn't rare for a gardener to lose an entire bed to a tricky pest. Adding some netting around the beds can help to repel most critters but it doesn't look particularly appealing to the eye. Often, raised bed gardeners will find themselves waiting until they have a problem before they start to fix it. But when you are picking a location, you can keep in mind entryways for critters to get into your garden so that you know where you can cut off access with the least amount of hassle.

By keeping track of these features of your space, you will equip yourself with all of the information you need to plan what to grow in your raised bed garden. It's almost time to start seeding your garden but first there are a couple more things you should consider as you plan out the placement of your beds.

RAISED BED GARDENING

First, though we've mentioned it previously, you need to remember that the width of your raised bed is very important. You shouldn't make it any wider than four feet or you will diminish the level of care that you can give to the plants in the center. Keep it under four feet wide but make it longer if you are looking to do a large bed. The length can go on forever but the width should be kept below four feet.

Also consider how many beds you are planning to place in the location. If you are just doing a single one then this doesn't matter but if you are doing more than one you should take a moment to consider their distance from each other and the room for you to walk around them when it comes time to tend. You should keep a foot or two between beds in order to not crowd up your space. If you drop below this then you are raising the chances that some flowers don't get properly tended to because reaching them is difficult. Also consider mowing your walkway and laying down some dirt or cobblestones. This will help to make the area around your raised garden beds less prone to weeds. While raised garden beds deal with weeds far less often than regular garden beds do, reducing the chances of an infestation even further is always a smart idea.

One last thing to keep in mind is how family and friends will respond to the placement. If you have children then you should be mindful of where they like to play and how this might affect them or how they might affect the raised garden bed. Lower beds are at risk of being trampled if a stray baseball gets lost among the vegetation. Also consider what plant matter might fall into the raised bed from trees above and note any branches that might need to be trimmed back or are at risk of falling. Everything in your raised bed garden could be perfect from the temperature to the amount of sun, the drainage of the soil, and the protection from the wind, but a falling branch or the feet of a rampaging child can quickly destroy a garden and make all of the effort for naught.

While this can be a lot to take in and consider, it is well worth the time. If you are reading a book on gardening then you are pretty much ready to get started and you must be excited. So saying slow down probably doesn't sound like much fun. But a well placed raised bed garden can last your entire life with a little bit of care. A poorly placed raised bed might not even last you a single season. It pays to be mindful and attentive when planning so that everything goes smoothly.

Make sure you test several different spots; you never know what might be perfect for a lettuce crop and what might be perfect for some tomatoes instead. Or some raspberries, or strawberries, roses, rosemary, or mint. There are tons of options when it comes to what you can grow in your raised garden beds coming up in the next chapter. But first, since we've gone through all of the effort of picking the perfect spot for our beds, let's sow some seeds and start them growing.

How to Plant Your Raised Bed Garden

If you don't already know what you are going to grow in your raised garden bed then there will be plenty of ideas for you in the next chapter. But if you already know then you don't need to wait any longer, it is time to plant them. Though you still need to make a couple decisions on how you want to do this. First off you will need to decide if you want to plant seeds into your raised garden bed or if you want to start seeds individually to transplant seedlings to the raised bed. If you decide on sowing seeds directly then you have a couple choices on how to do it. We'll cover these first then learn everything there is to know about transplanting seedlings into your outdoor beds.

Starting from seeds, there are a few things to consider. First, remember that you can't plant them into the ground until after the last frost of the winter. Also remember that you shouldn't sow seeds when it is raining out. You can choose whether you want to pay special attention to the sowing step or not but raised garden beds will make the process quicker and easier than it normally is. That said, you should also avoid sowing seeds during windy weather as well since seeds can easily blow away depending on their needs.

How deeply you plant your seeds and how much soil you cover them with afterwards is going to differ between species. Some seeds like to be buried half an inch under the soil but there are others which need the energy from direct sunlight in order to germinate properly. If these were buried under the soil then they would never fully grow into seedlings because they wouldn't have the energy to break out of the shell. In general though, most seeds are going to want to be half an inch to a quarter inch below the surface of the soil. Regardless of depth, almost every type of seed imaginable likes to be watered deeply after it is planted. When planting an entire bed, fully sow the seeds before moving on to watering.

RAISED BED GARDENING

You seed most garden beds one of two ways. On the careful side you drop a couple seeds into small holes you made in the soil. These are spaced out and weaker plants are trimmed back shortly after sprouting so that each plant has a bit of space around it to grow. The other way that is often used is to take a hoe and dig out a line from one end of the bed to the next. This is repeated as desired, allowing for half a foot to a foot of space between each row depending on the space needs of the intended plant. Seeds are dropped throughout this groove and then the hoe is used to cover it all over. This doesn't offer the same level of control over the placement of the final plants but it keeps everything mostly in a row. If you were doing this directly into the soil then you would also be mixing up and spreading weed seeds while doing this. But in a raised garden bed you don't have this problem. In fact, a raised garden bed offers a third way of sowing seeds that is beginner friendly, though it can be a bit messy.

Since a raised garden bed is filled up with soil that you put there, you know that there aren't any weeds in it and so there is no problem with mixing it up even further. Everything is contained within the bed, so you can throw handfuls of seeds around as you like and then take a hoe and just run through the bed a couple times to make sure everything is mixed up and buried. With no hassle at all, you can sow an entire bed this way. Of course, this is best used when the raised bed is going to be one kind of plant. If you are mixing and matching species in the bed then this will only lead to more mix-ups and weird placements.

That's pretty much all there is to sowing seeds directly into the raised garden bed. Though you will need to thin out the seedlings as they come up, regardless of which method you take. In fact, even when you start seeds indoors you will still find yourself in a situation in which you need to remove some seedlings. Some species, like lettuce, can be eaten when they are still a seedling but most of the time we're simply removing plants that are no longer useful to us. It might seem weird at first but there is only so much room in a single bed and we want to make sure our plants get as much nutrients as they can to stay healthy and produce large harvests and beautiful colors.

Speaking of starting plants indoors, carefully germinating seeds and growing strong seedlings prior to taking the plants outdoors is actually a really great way to get a head start on the season since you can get three-week-old seedlings into the ground the day after the last frost. Of course, it takes more time, effort, and money to start seeds indoors but depending on how you approach gardening, it may be well worth the investment. Seeds shouldn't cost more than a couple dollars. You will need some soil but we'll just start with a version of our raised bed soil that is a little lighter on the compost. You'll want to get some plastic wrap, perhaps a spray bottle for water. All of that shouldn't cost more than $20. But unfortunately you'll also want to get an LED grow light and this will run $80 on the low end. But LED lights will save you money in the long run because they don't need to be replaced as often and then don't take much electricity. Just make sure the one you purchase is designed for growing vegetables because regular LED lights just won't cut it there. When you have all these pieces, you can start your seeds.

Fill up the small seeding containers with the soil mixture. We use a similar mixture to the soil in our raised garden beds so that transplanting isn't as hard on the plants. However, we use less compost in our mixture because we are working with smaller plants and we don't want to overfeed them. We will give them liquid fertilizer once a week but this will also be at only half or a quarter the strength that we feed our raised garden beds.

Once the containers are all filled, get your seeds ready by planting them each individually. Just use a finger to dig a half inch hole in the soil and drop some seeds. Depending on the size of the plastic trays you are using this could be done only once or twice each container. Drop a few seeds into each hole rather than only one. Some seeds will fail to germinate and so it is always better to have too many seedlings that you need to remove rather than no seedlings at all. Cover or leave the seeds open to the air depending on the type but either way you will want to water the soil entirely. Make sure that water is running throughout the whole of the soil rather than just along the top. Finally, take your plastic wrap and cover up the top of the container then place it under your grow light. How many hours of light they get will depend on what species you are growing.

The plastic wrap is placed over the container to help keep the humidity up. Some plants don't like a lot of humidity but it is pretty much the regular for any vegetables you might be growing. As the seeds are germinating, you are going to want to remove the plastic wrap at least twice a day. One time is to spray water onto the soil with the spray bottle you purchased for exactly that reason. The second time is simply to offer more air to get to the roots of the plant. You might consider using a toothpick to poke holes in the plastic wrap to allow air in. The level of humidity won't stay as high but it might be beneficial to trade a little humidity for oxygen. When spraying with water you only need to soak the top inch. Watering will change after the seedling starts to sprout so pay attention to it. Once it starts to touch the plastic wrap or grow its first set of leaves, whichever happens first, remove the plastic wrap and move onto the next stage. Seeds may take a couple days or a few weeks to reach this stage depending on the species.

After the plastic wrap is off, you will water your seedlings as is needed. Use a finger to test the top inch of the soil to see if it is dry. When it is, water the seedlings thoroughly. Remember that they aren't very strong yet so water the soil and not the plants themselves. You wouldn't want the water to break a stem or anything. You will need to fertilize them once a week but you should dilute the fertilizer mixture with water so it is only a quarter as strong. Seedlings will typically take two or three weeks to be ready but some take much more. As a rule of thumb, seedlings are ready to be transplanted once they start developing their second set of leaves. However, before you can move an indoor plant into an outdoor raised garden bed, you are going to need to take a week to harden it off.

Hardening off plants is done to prepare indoor plants for a life outside. When they are raised indoors, plants have no reason to develop natural protection from wind and sunlight that they grow when they are started outdoors. You should find a place outside with full shade and protection from the wind. Put the plants outside in this spot for an hour on the first day. Put them out for two hours the second day, three hours the next. Do this over the course of a week, moving the plant into more and more sunlight slowly through the week. This will get the plant used to the outside and it should only take a week for it to start developing natural protections so it can thrive outdoors. After a week of hardening off, it will be time to transplant your seedlings into the raised bed garden.

When seedlings are ready to transplant, make sure you don't move them into the garden until after any wind or rain has stopped and the raised garden bed has a chance to dry out a little. It is best to transplant seedlings early in the morning. Since we have to thoroughly water seedlings after planting, it is best to transplant them early so that there is plenty of time for the water to evaporate before the evening. You should also stop watering your seedlings prior to planting. In fact, you shouldn't water them during the hardening off period except to provide a spray or two of water if they start to wilt too much. Transplanting seedlings is pretty much a dry soil experience.

RAISED BED GARDENING

Take your seedling container and hold two fingers against the base of the plant. Grip it firmly while you rotate and flip over the plant pot. Do this over a bucket or outside so that you don't have to worry about potting soil getting all over the place. As the soil falls out, you should start to see the roots of the seedling. Try not to damage these or to sit them down on any surface you haven't cleaned yet. It is very important to replace these roots carefully but first we should check them to make sure that the seedling is healthy. Roots that are in good health will be white or light brown and those that are infected and rotting will not only be black but they'll also be covered in a slimy residue. This is a sign of root rot from overwatering your seedlings. If you catch it early then you can remove the infected roots before introducing the plant to your raised garden bed. If it hasn't spread to the foliage yet then this will save your plant's life. Always check the roots when transplanting. It isn't good for a plant's health to be digging it up to check the roots and so you should always take a chance to look them over when they are going to be exposed anyway.

You want to plant your seedlings into the raised garden bed so that they're roughly the same height as they were in their original container. You will want to dig out a little hole in the soil to set the roots into. Carefully cover the roots with soil and pack it in tightly around the base of the plant's stem to keep it firm and not wobbling around. Water the seedling fully and then check on it over the next couple days. It might look a little weak at first but you should see it start to stand up tall and grow strong. It is a good idea to transplant seedlings about halfway between receiving fertilizer and the following application. This will allow the soil enough time to dry out so that fertilizing and watering can continue as usual.

Starting your seeds indoors may make for a lot more work but the rewards speak for themselves. Bigger plants at the start of the growing season can result in large yields or even an extra harvest but that comes at the cost of a LED grow light and the time it takes to properly germinate seeds and put them through hardening off and transplanting. If you have the time and resources to do it, starting indoors is the way to go but that doesn't mean sowing directly into the ground is necessarily a bad idea. It can have results in the same range for much less effort but it does invite more randomness and chances for error where indoor starting offers gardeners more control over the process. Ultimately, you will have to decide for yourself which is the right way to go when it comes to your raised bed gardens.

RAISED BED GARDENING

Chapter Summary

- When you plant a raised bed garden is going to be determined on the temperature of where you live and what you want to plant.

- Plants that want warmer weather will need to wait longer to plant.

- Most plants like to go in the ground after the last frost of the winter, once the soil is warm enough. Most of the plants we grow in a raised bed garden are killed by frost. Not all of them, but enough to make it a general rule.

- If you are growing in your raised garden bed from seed then you will need to start after the last frost. If you are starting indoors and then transplanting the seedlings you will want to start them a few weeks before the last frost so they get in the ground quickly.

- Most plants are going to want the soil temperature to be at least 60F. There are some like lettuce which can go into the ground while it is much colder but 60F covers most. Use a soil thermometer to watch for the right time. You will find that a raised garden bed is ready earlier in the year than a ground-based bed.

- It is important not to plant seeds or transplant seedlings if it has been raining. You always want to plant your garden when it is dry, never when it is wet.

- Most plants will want to go into the ground in the spring and come out in the fall. But there are some, like lettuce and other leafy greens, which can go through several harvests in a season and be replanted. It all depends on the growing period of your plants.

- You can place a raised bed garden anywhere you want but then you will be limited in your choice of plants. You will only be able to grow ones that enjoy those environmental conditions.

- It is better to consider the location of your garden carefully, to keep track of how much sunlight it gets throughout the day. Keeping track of information like this will help you to finetune your placement for the plants you want to grow.

- If you want to grow both full sun and partial shade plants then your best bet is using more than one raised garden bed rather than try to get them both to work together in one.

- You should also consider the natural draining of your chosen location and how the temperature changes between day and night. Raising the garden bed will help with draining but areas at the bottom of hills will still end up holding onto a lot more moisture. The temperature of the soil in the ground will be a little lower than a raised garden bed but this will give you a good idea of what you are working with.

- Also take into account protection from wind, rain, or critters. What about branches overhead or other objects that could fall and damage the garden bed? All of these should be noted and written down when picking a spot.

- Never make garden beds more than four feet wide, as this will lead to neglected plants.

- Be careful to place your raised garden beds in locations that don't have a lot of foot traffic. Trampled garden beds don't produce many plants.

- Take your time and consider a few locations before deciding on the ones that work the best to meet your plants' needs.

- How deeply you sow seeds in the soil of your raised bed garden is going to be determined by the seeds themselves. Some seeds like to be buried with soil and others like to be exposed to the sun.

- In general, you will hoe the garden and deposit the seeds in that way. Water seeds after they have been planted. As seedlings come up, you remove the weaker ones to give the plants enough space to grow.

- Starting your plants indoors will allow you to get seedlings into the ground right after the last frost. This gives you a two or three week head start on your plants.

- Starting seeds indoors requires suitable containers, plastic wrap, and LED grow lights.

- Fill up the containers with soil then deposit a few seeds in a small hole. Water them deeply and then cover them with plastic wrap. Set them under the LED grow lights for a period of time determined by the species being grown. Take the plastic wrap off twice a day to let oxygen in and mist the soil daily. Remove the plastic wrap after seedlings begin to sprout their first set of leaves.

- When seedlings begin to grow their second set of leaves, it is time to harden them off in preparation for transplanting. Set plants outdoors for an hour on the first day in a spot that has full shade and protection from the wind. Add an hour to this time on day two and slowly move it into partial shade. Do this for a week, adding another hour each day and letting the plant get more direct sunlight. This will cause it to develop protections to survive outdoors.

- After a week of hardening off, remove seedlings from their containers while being careful with the roots. Look for black and slimy roots that are a sign of rot. Remove any you find. Transplant seedlings by setting their roots in the soil of the raised garden bed, packing them in tightly and then watering them fully.

- Seedlings will continue to grow healthily in the raised garden bed if they are properly hardened off and transplanted. This can give you a jump on the growing season or even just help to ensure that seeds germinate properly.

In the next chapter you will learn about all the different species of plants that take well to growing in raised beds. These range from different garden veggies such as leafy greens like lettuce or spinach, through to tomatoes, onions, or even potatoes. They also make a great space for herbs like basil, rosemary, or thyme. Plus, for those more concerned with the aesthetics of gardening, they look lovely when filled with bright and beautiful flowers of all kinds.

CHAPTER FOUR

WHAT TO PLANT IN YOUR RAISED BED GARDEN

If you haven't yet figured out what you want to grow in your raised bed garden then this chapter is for you. There are a lot of options available to you, though the primary factor limiting them is your local climate. You won't be able to grow plants that need tons of sun if you don't have much and instead live in a colder area. However, once you move past this obstacle then you will find that there are plenty of plants that do great in a raised bed.

A raised garden bed is pretty much exactly the same as a regular garden bed but with some added benefits such as better drainage. If you could grow a plant in the ground in your local area then you can grow it in a raised bed garden. However, there are some plants that do better in a raised bed than the ground. One example is succulents. These plants come from hot and dry areas and they like to have a soil that is very sandy, even to the point of being rocky. While too much moisture will rot just about any plant's roots, succulents are especially prone to it. The added draining speed that comes from raising up a garden bed for succulents will help them to survive and thrive much easier than if they were just in the ground. In fact, if you are going to grow succulents at all then I absolutely suggest either a raised bed or an elevated position in the ground if possible.

But succulents are just one (beautiful) example of what you can grow in a raised garden bed. This chapter is filled with tons of others ranging from flowers to veggies and everything in between.

The Best Vegetables for a Raised Bed Garden

Raised garden beds are a fantastic choice for most vegetables. The extra drainage and the reduced risk of pests make raised beds an easier experience for beginners looking to start their first vegetable garden, as well as those who have been at it for years. As long as you provide some protection against critters like deer, raising up the beds you grow your vegetables in is pretty much your best bet if you have issues with aphids and other pest infestations. Plus, you reduce the risk of disease through the added drainage and you can make sure that no harmful chemicals enter the soil from nearby sources. If you are looking to enjoy your own garden vegetables then a raised bed is the best choice for protection, reduction of disease, and control over the growing environment.

Plus, there are tons of veggies that absolutely thrive when given the extra space that a raised garden bed offers. Let's take a look at some of the standout veggies that love these gardens.

Raised beds offer the best way to grow root vegetables like sweet potatoes or turnips. Sweet potatoes in particular are a great fit for a raised bed vegetable garden since they are packed full of fiber, manganese, vitamins A and C, and a ton of antioxidants. Turnips on the other hand are a great source for fiber, manganese, potassium, and vitamin C, plus they have even been tentatively linked to reducing the risk for certain kinds of cancer. Other options for tasty root vegetables include beets, radishes, fennel, and carrots. Of course, potatoes are also a root vegetable and could fit in this list but we'll be looking at them specifically in a moment because raised beds offer them an even greater benefit. For now, let us consider why root vegetables categorically do better in raised garden beds.

Aside from the additional help in draining, raised garden beds also provide plenty of controlled space for the roots of your plants. If you are only a foot off the ground then you might not have as much space as necessary for root vegetables in your raised garden bed but once you go up to a foot and a half or more, root vegetables will love it. When you plant in the ground, you need to trust that the soil in the ground will support your vegetables. We change out a good deal of the soil and replace it with our own but normal soil presses in on all sides of our garden bed. It is very easy for a root vegetable to grow large enough it pushes into this soil. You can't be sure what is down there if you haven't dug it up. One major issue that arises from this are rocks in the soil which cause root vegetables to grow misshapen and deformed. When you plant in a raised bed, you know that you have several feet of nutritious soil to support your veggies as they mature. Root vegetables that are grown in a raised garden bed tend to have larger yields because there are fewer castoffs harvested.

Potatoes will benefit from growing in a raised garden bed for the same reason. Root vegetables tend to be directly connected to the above soil part, making it easy to harvest them. Carrots, for example, are harvested by brushing back the soil around their top and then yanking them out. Turnips will show the shoulders of the turnip itself above the surface, so you can easily tell what size it is. Potatoes are a little different though. The leafy green part above the surface is connected to the potato below through what looks almost like an electrical wire. This could grow straight down but more often it will bend or take a wavy path through the soil. The potato will grow at the end of this cord, which means that you could have a potato directly beneath the above soil part but more often it is to one of the sides. Potatoes may go deep under the soil and require a bunch of digging, or they may be up near the top. This makes it very easy to slice open potatoes when you are trying to dig them up for harvest.

A raised garden bed takes care of this problem, thankfully. You know exactly how much space the potato has to grow and you can start from the walls and move inwards as you remove soil. This will cause the soil closer to the plant to start to fall away and you can use gravity to do most of the digging for you. Less digging means there is a smaller chance that you slice open your potatoes when you go to harvest them. Just keep in mind that potatoes like loose soil and so you should add some sand to your raised garden bed soil mixture if you are looking to plant your own. This does limit the types of veggies that you can grow alongside your potatoes but raised garden beds are known for producing larger yields of massive potatoes, which makes them a great plant to grow if you are looking to add food to your table or veggies to sell at the local farmer's market.

Lettuce and spinach make for another excellent choice for a raised garden bed but for entirely different reasons. These leafy greens, and others like them, don't actually need much space for their roots. They have quick shallow systems, so even a half a foot raised garden bed will benefit them. However, you will probably want to go a little bit higher to offer faster drainage since leafy greens don't like having a lot of moisture around their roots. They are prone to rotting, so a foot tall or more is recommended. While leafy greens do better in a hydroponic system than they do in soil, they do better in a raised garden bed when compared to the ground. The extra drainage is largely responsible for this but there is one secret to their success and why you find them in so many raised bed gardens.

Remember that lettuce and leafy greens in general are one of those crops which can be harvested a couple times a year if you time it correctly. It is also important to take note of the fact that lettuce can withstand much lower temperatures compared to many other garden vegetables. This means that if you are growing in the ground, lettuce will be one of the crops you plant earliest. If you plant straight from seed, you can normally get two harvests in a season. You might be able to squeeze a third one in when you start your lettuce plants as transplants. But this is a little different when you are using raised bed gardens. When you take soil readings to make sure that it is warm enough to start planting, take a moment and compare the temperature of your raised garden bed to the ground soil. You'll see that the raised garden bed has slightly warmer soil compared to the ground. The elevated height helps it to warm up faster and this means you can plant your vegetables sooner. If you are planting lettuce then this advantage will let you harvest between three to four times in the season, though one of those harvests will be primarily microgreens. The real limiting factor here is how early the first frost of the year comes. If it is a later one then you'll be able to get a lot of lettuce out of a raised bed garden.

Tomatoes are best grown in spaced out grid formations rather than in rows like many vegetables are. Raised garden beds are easy to divide up and a four-by-eight bed bed will give you enough space to grow eight tomato plants. You will need to add some wiring or trellis in order to help support the vines and the weight of the fruits but this can actually double as critter protection if you set it up properly. While potatoes prefer to have more minerals in their soil, tomatoes rely on lots of nutrients as they are very hungry plants that require lots of healthy additions to their soil. The primary way of supporting them in this fashion will be to provide ample fertilizer but increasing the amount of compost in the soil will also be necessary. This will result in a soil that isn't overly strong, so it can take a little bit of effort to get a trellis or a cage to properly stand, but running a line of wire around the cages after they have been set up will create a tight hold that uses the natural resistance of the cages to keep everything in place.

Cucumbers are another vegetable that do great in a raised bed. While cucumbers need lots of watering, they don't like having a lot of moisture sticks around in the soil. The faster draining that comes from using a raised bed garden will go a long way towards keeping your cucumbers nice and healthy. You will want to treat them like tomatoes and attach them to a trellis or a cage, though they don't need their soil to be quite so mineral-heavy. It is best to grow cucumbers in their own beds rather than mixed in with other vegetables. They need lots of space and they can turn a garden bed into a mess real quick.

Onions do particularly well in raised beds. Again, they like the quick draining speed. But onions, as well as similar veggies like leeks, like to have lots of nitrogen in their soil. This isn't a feature shared with many vegetables. They all like having some nitrogen but onions like having a lot. Too much can be harmful to certain species so be careful when researching your onions. You don't want them to share a bed with something like cucumbers, peas, or carrots, all vegetables which don't like very much nitrogen.

Zucchini plants do well in the ground and in a raised bed, and while a raised garden bed won't really affect the yield size very much, it can make zucchini a much easier plant to grow. Zucchinis tend to produce massive harvests but part of this is due to the way they almost act like weeds. Zucchinis like to stretch out and spread all throughout a bed. You may plant some zucchini in a garden bed alongside other veggies, only to come back and find out your garden is now overrun with zucchinis and the other plants aren't getting enough nutrients to stay healthy. Growing zucchini in a raised bed garden will fix this issue, though you should keep them to their own bed or you'll just be recreating the conditions necessary for the problem you were solving.

These are just the vegetables that stand out the most. The truth of the matter is that pretty much everything either grows well or better in a raised bed garden rather than in the ground. It offers better drainage, more protection, and a higher level of control over the growing environment. The only way to get better control is to switch over to indoor hydroponics or greenhouse growing. This level of control doesn't come without some upkeep. It takes a lot of work to keep a garden in good shape and we'll be covering that in the next chapter. But first, let's take a look at some of the flowers used to make beautiful and aesthetically pleasing raised bed displays.

Using Your Raised Beds for Flowers

Raised beds aren't just for growing delicious and nutritious vegetables. One of the reasons that they are so popular is the simple fact that they can look quite beautiful. With a little bit of time and tender care, a raised bed can be made to look like a natural part of the landscape or even used as a beautiful decoration. It can be filled with flowers of all different colors. This can be used to line pathways or create designs that are beautiful and captivating. It takes a little bit of time and effort but many flowers can be planted and grown year after year. You can choose to go with long-lasting ones or single season flowers, depending on how much energy you want to invest in the process.

What you plant is going to depend on what colors you want, as well as what season you want it to be the brightest. We'll look at an example of a beautiful and bright display for spring, summer, and fall to see some of the gorgeous flowers that you can use in your raised beds. Keep in mind that this is just an example of one arrangement you could go with but there are even more options for flowers than there are with vegetables. You will need to consider your local climate when choosing species but you'll find yourself with shocking amounts of variety.

Starting with spring, we'll grow a mixture of tazetta and jonquil-type daffodils. Tazetta have wide flower petals which peel back to crown the golden center that protrudes outwards. They are a striking flower when they are healthy and they compliment a jonquil-type daffodil quite nicely since these daffodils have white flower petals that sometimes come in yellow with bright yellow centers. Together, these two can create the main section of a bed. The bed will need to be at least a foot deep in order to support the root system. You can add some hellebores to the bed, which often have a deep purple color. Spread throughout a raised garden bed full of tazettas, these hellebores will really pop out in bold fashion.

Maintaining a spring bed of this fashion isn't very hard. You'll want this to be a partly shaded bed, with the hellebores getting the most shade. Both hellebores and tazetta are perennials and so you can keep these beds alive for several years. Pay attention to the tazetta and trim away any heads that die or that have faded too much. The hellebores will help to distract from the fading of the tazetta but if you remove the fading ones it will promote new growth and keep the bed bright. You will want to dig up the tazetta every few years to space them out a little more and reorganize the garden and keep the root system from becoming too tangled up. Keep an eye on watering and add a little bit of fertilizer from time to time and you will have yourself a gorgeous spring arrangement.

For a beautiful summer arrangement, plant a mixture of coreopsis, annual cosmos, and catmint. This will create a really strong contrast in the colors and a more three dimensional texture due to the height disparity. Catmint is the easier to pronounce name for nepeta mussinii. It is similar to its more well known cousin catnip, aka nepeta cataria. But catmint produces tall stems which bloom deep purple flowers from soil to tip. Mixing these in with coreopsis will create the color contrast, since coreopsis are mostly yellow petals around a yellow core. Some types of coreopsis will have dark red, almost black, rings around their center but otherwise they are pure yellow. To bring the arrangement together, some purple or pink annual cosmos are added. These have a shape closer to the coreopsis but a color like the catmint and so when added they create a sense of unity to the arrangement.

Again, this arrangement is made up of perennials which will last you several years if properly tended. To keep them bright and beautiful you will need to use fertilizer on them with a regular schedule. You will also need to trim back heads which have faded in color. Removing the heads will cause the flowers to bloom again, but this also helps keep the plant healthy and happy in general. It both makes your raised bed garden look better and helps your plant to better distribute its energy. The annual cosmos will need to be replanted every year but you can use this as a chance to switch up the colors and try something new. The annual cosmos can also be replaced with another perennial if desired, which will reduce the amount of upkeep required on the raised bed each year.

For fall, we are going to go with similar colors to summer but our purples will be darker and our lighter shades will be a little bit more washed out in appearance. Washed out flowers might not sound appealing at first but keep in mind that we're talking about fall, that season where the colors turn deep oranges and reds before fading out. A washed out flower actually fits with the season perfectly to deepen that natural mood that autumn invokes. For this washed out look we will use sedum and goldenrod. We set this off against the deep purple shades of asters to create a really rich and moody display.

It should be noted that the sedum is a succulent and this works well for a quick discussion about winter. There aren't many flowers that enjoy the winter weather but there are a few succulents which are planted in fall to grow throughout the winter. These can keep a raised bed garden looking beautiful throughout the winter, which is especially useful for raised beds that work as pathways or those seeded with annuals. Some winter succulents that are beautiful include the green and purple royanum, the broad and bold agave, the unique cobweb sempervivum, the rose-like jovibarba, and the adorable orostachys. These are just a few of the succulents that can make your raised bed gardens stand out even in the coldest of weather.

Growing Herbs in a Raised Garden Bed

The best way to grow herbs, if you want the most plentiful and aromatic herbs possible, is to use a hydroponic system. However, failing this, the second best way is to use a raised garden bed. There are tons of delicious and nutritious herbs that you can grow in a raised flower bed. Doing so will save you between a little to a lot of money, depending on how often you use herbs in your cooking. If you haven't started using herbs as you cook, growing your own can be a great way to get started. Simply choose one of the plants in this section, start growing it, and google some recipes that use it. You'll be amazed at how much flavor can be packed into such a small serving.

Before we look at the herbs themselves, it is worth taking a moment to think about where we are growing our herbs. If you have a window ledge raised garden bed by the kitchen window, you can tend to your herbs and pick them fresh for every meal. The further away they are, the less you'll want to do this. What generally happens is gardeners take a few clippings while tending the raised bed but mostly the herbs are harvested together at the end of the season. Window ledge beds will provide fresh herbs without needing to leave the house and this leads to them being picked much more often. This in turn promotes the herbs to grow more and it makes for a high yielding investment. You can use the herbs throughout the season and then harvest and preserve them at the end.

While you will want to double check all of the growing requirements of the following, you will notice that most of them can be grown together. This is fantastic because it allows you to bring a lot of flavor and variety into your garden with even a single raised bed. Herbs also spread out and take up a lot of space but they have a tendency to cluster well together. Plus, the smell will be wonderful. Especially if you go with something very aromatic like mint. It goes great with ice cream or in a tea, plus it helps to keep your breath smelling great. Not only that but there's a reason that products like Tums come in a mint flavor; it actually helps to calm the stomach and reduce heartburn. Just be careful with mint, as it likes to spread the most out of any of the herbs and so you need to be careful of how much space you let it take up in your raised bed.

If you are looking to eat healthier then herbs a fantastic way to go. Plant some rosemary and oregano near the kitchen. Far from the only nutritious cooking herbs, they are among the healthiest ingredients you could add to a meal. Rosemary is a source for iron, calcium, and vitamin B6. Oregano is even more packed since it is a source of fiber, iron, manganese, tryptophan, omega fatty acid, calcium, and vitamin E. That's one of those plants that are so good for you, your fingers get tired typing all of their benefits! These are far from the only herbs used in cooking, but most of them fall into a different category. Rosemary and oregano are most noteworthy for what they add to your diet. They don't have the same health benefits in the way that mint does. But that opens up a whole other reason you may want to grow herbs: medicinal purposes.

While "medicinal herb" may sound like a code word for cannabis, it actually describes a whole lot of herbs you've heard of that are secretly super beneficial to us. Mint, thyme, cilantro, parsley, sage, chives, and basil are all members of this category that can also be added to meals. But for now we'll worry about their benefits rather than their flavors. We already looked at mint and saw that it helps to settle upset stomachs, but the rest of these are just as useful to have around.

Coffee might be the most well known diuretic but thyme is pretty close on that list. If you are having urinary problems, a little thyme in your diet might just help you get over that. But more than this, thyme also helps to fight off bacteria and so adding it to your diet can help to keep you free from bacteria-based illnesses. Basil, on the other hand, is another delicious herb that is commonly used in dishes as varied as country style shepherd's pie or Italian pasta. But it actually helps to reduce inflammation and adding it to your diet can help to reduce arthritis pain. Sage has been linked to an improvement in memory, plus it also helps to reduce pain from inflammation and swelling.

If you have problems with cholesterol or high blood pressure then you should consider growing chives. Studies are still being conducted but so far they point towards chives have a positive effect in lowering these two issues. We'll learn more as research progresses but for the time being they are delicious enough to make a great addition to a raised herb garden to be included. Parsley is a little bit like mint in that it will make your breath smell better but it is also good for flushing out heavy metals from your body. We try to avoid getting too many of these, which is one of the reasons we are careful not to use building materials like railroad ties when constructing our raised garden beds. Cilantro is also great for this, though it doesn't leave your breath nearly as fresh as parsley does.

Regardless of whether or not you want to grow herbs for their medical properties, their nutrition value, or their taste, they are a fantastic crop and your life will benefit from growing your own in a raised bed garden you built with your own two hands.

Chapter Summary

- Raised bed gardens are great fits for many types of plants. They are particularly useful for vegetables, flowers, and herbs.

- Growing vegetables in a raised bed is a great way to reduce the risk of disease and harmful chemicals from getting into your food. You will need to protect yourself from hungry critters but who can blame them, vegetables grown this way taste amazing.

- Root vegetables grow particularly well in a raised bed garden. Sweet potatoes and turnips are just two of the many examples you could go with. The extra depth offered from a raised bed garden allows for root vegetables to grow deeply without having to worry about hitting rocks that cause deformities.

- One of the big issues with harvesting potatoes is damaging them during the removal process. By digging out the soil against the wall of the raised bed garden, you can use gravity to help you displace the dirt and find your potatoes without worrying about damaging them.

- Lettuce, spinach, and leafy greens in general are great picks for raised bed gardens. They don't need much room for their roots but they are prone to rotting and so the drainage speed of a raised bed garden is perfect for them. You can grow leafy greens to harvest several times in a single season, making them a great choice if you love salads.

- Tomatoes need to be spaced out and provided with a trellis but a raised bed garden can easily offer you space to grow a few plants.

- Cucumbers don't like having too much moisture in the soil and so a raised garden bed is a particularly enjoyable experience for them.

- Onions are like cucumbers but they like having more nitrogen in their diet than most plants do.

- Zucchinis do well but they can easily take over a garden bed so you should only grow them in their own raised bed.

- There are a ton of options for what types of flowers you can grow in a raised bed garden. You can choose to grow annuals that need to be replaced each year but growing a base of returning perennials with annuals spread throughout offers a less time-intensive alternative.

- When deciding on flowers, you need to decide if you want them to be the prettiest in the spring, the summer, or the fall. This will determine which species you go with.

- Consider the way that the colors, heights, and textures of flowers interact with each other. A great way to make things blend is to have a flower which connects the others in the bed. If you have a tall purple flower and a small white flower, getting a flower the size of one but the color of the other will tie the entire bed together.

- Fresh herbs taste absolutely amazing when you add them to your cooking. The best way to get the freshest herbs is to grow them yourself with a window ledge raised bed garden. Open up your window, pluck some fresh herbs, and add them straight to your dishes without leaving the kitchen.

- Pretty much all herbs taste amazing but we can eat them to improve our diets. Rosemary is full of iron, calcium, and vitamin B6. Organo is packed with even more elements of a healthy diet.

- But we also grow and eat herbs for medical reasons. Mint helps with digestion. Basil helps reduce inflammation. Sage is used to improve memory. There are a whole bunch of medical reasons to add herbs to your diet. They're both tasty and super great for you, plus they do well in a raised bed garden.

In the next chapter you will learn how to maintain your raised bed garden so that it continues to produce plenty of delicious plants or beautiful flowers. Questions ranging from the best soil to the most appropriate fertilizer will be covered, as well as how to deal with pests should the need arise, when and how to water your raised bed garden, and what to do if weeds start popping up.

CHAPTER FIVE

MAINTAINING YOUR RAISED BED GARDEN

Once you have seeded your raised bed garden and have raised the seedlings into young plants, you are still going to need to pay careful attention to your plants and their needs. As the gardener looking after these beds it is up to you to properly water and fertilize your plants. It is up to you to repair the frame and amend the soil. And it is up to you to watch out for pests and to prevent disease from entering into your garden. While you could skip these steps, your garden won't stay healthy unless you follow through with them all. You will need to get a feel for your garden and come up with a schedule that works for you but even more important is that it works for your plants.

But while all of these are necessary, they aren't difficult. In fact, raised bed gardens are easier to maintain than traditional gardens are and depending on the size of your beds you may not even have to bend down to work on them anymore. The height of a raised bed makes it easier to maintain and the contained environment means there is less that needs to be checked. But there is no such thing as a 100% maintenance-free garden. We'll figure out how to maintain ours starting with the soil before moving on to fertilizing, watering, and pest protection.

Amending the Soil

As gardeners, our goal should be to keep our garden as healthy as can be so that it continues to produce fantastic results year after year. But doing this shouldn't mean spending a lot of money. A little bit of attention from time to time will allow you to keep the same soil in your raised garden bed for years without a problem. To look after our soil, we're going to amend it occasionally and make sure it is protected throughout the winter. By taking care of it before the start of winter and just after the end, you'll be able to keep your soil healthy for many seasons to come. You should still check on the quality of the soil when you can but this won't be necessary when the following steps are heeded.

When we mixed up our soil for our raised beds, we start from a base of 33% compost. This means that there are lots of nutrients in our garden soil to begin with. But as each harvest passes, there are going to be fewer and fewer nutrients in the soil. You should add compost either after you finish harvesting or in early spring when you start to prepare the beds. You will only need to do this once a year, otherwise you could overload your soil. While this is one way to get lots of nutrients into the soil, we'll also be using a liquid fertilizer in a few moments and this will ensure that there are tons of nutrients available to the plants.

But it is important to realize that there is such a thing as too many nutrients. When you or I eat, we stop after we get full. Plants can't do this. If there are too many nutrients in the soil then they may suffer nutrient burn. The edges of leaves will gradually curl up like the legs of a dead spider and it'll start to change colors. It's an ugly sight. If you start to see signs of nutrient burn then you should slow down and use less fertilizer. You may need to check the pH level of the garden bed to make sure it is still within the proper levels that it was supposed to be. If there are too many nutrients then you will want to water as normal but skip a fertilizer application or two so that the soil is flushed out a bit first.

The organic elements in the soil will break down over time. When this happens, they start to stick together much tighter and the pathways through the soil start to get blocked up. This makes the soil tougher for roots to push through while also blocking access to oxygen and slowing down the drainage speed. As you water your garden throughout the first year, be mindful of how long it takes to dry out and the way the water soaks into it. When you first start, it will seem a little odd to be watching the water this closely but over time it will tell you about the quality of the soil. When it starts to slow down and really change, typically after two years or more, then you will know what is happening. At the beginning of the new growing season, you can either amend the soil by adding more sandy minerals to it or you can replace the soil with a fresh batch. It can be expensive to constantly replace the soil every few years. Amending is the much cheaper way to go but you need to be careful and take it slow. You could completely wreck the soil if you added too much of one thing in without mixing it around and getting a feeling for the texture.

Winter is a big change in the weather and you need to prepare your raised garden beds to weather the storms. First off, most gardeners yank their plants out at the end of the season so that they can replant in the following spring. This is a good idea but you should only cut away the above-soil part of the plant. Remove any root vegetables as well but you want to leave the roots. Over the course of the winter they will turn into nutritious compost for your next crop. Speaking of compost, if you decide to add compost to the bed at the end of the growing season then you should make a layer of it on top, then cover this with a layer of mulch. This will make it so weeds can't get in, plus it will allow the compost to amend the soil and replenish many of the nutrients that were spent that summer.

If you aren't going to be mulching your raised garden beds then you should consider covering them using a strong plastic tarp. This will protect the soil and act in the place of mulch. It won't look quite as nice but if you are in an area where it snows a lot then you know that everything looks the same when it's buried in white fluff. It will be cheaper and far faster to put a tarp over your raised garden bed but mulching is the way to go if you are going to add compost before the winter. If you mulch, you can still use the tarp but it is rather redundant to use both methods.

By following these simple steps you can keep your soil lasting years. Checking on it throughout the season is important but making sure you prepare it for the winter and then "wake it up" again in the spring, it'll last you quite a while. The health of your soil is an investment well worth making. If you ignore it, you will find that it gets harder and harder to grow anything in your raised beds. You might think there is a problem with the bed while it is the soil at fault.

Fertilizing Your Raised Bed Garden

When you start seedlings indoors, you begin to fertilize them. When seedlings start to sprout outdoors, you fertilize them. As your plants grow and mature, you fertilize them. It is only just before you harvest any edible vegetables that you stop fertilizing them because you don't want to add any more liquid to the soil. Fertilizing your plants is an absolute must if you want beautiful flowers or large yields.

Fertilizer comes in two types. There are fertilizers such as manure which can be added to and then mixed throughout the soil. A fertilizer like this is a good application at the start of spring or end of fall. However, we can also mix in compost as a top layer with a blanket of mulch to protect our beds over the winter and add nutrients back into the soil. So we're not going to worry about fertilizers that mix into the soil. Instead, we're going to stick with liquid fertilizer.

There are many options when it comes to liquid fertilizers. Some gardeners brew what is called manure tea, which sounds as tasty as it smells. Another form of fertilizer is created by crushing comfrey until it oozes a sap which you distill in water and then feed your plants. For our purposes we will be sticking to the store bought liquid fertilizers but even here we have two options. The first option is to buy a premixed fertilizer. These are ones with the NPK ratio listed on them in numeric form like 30-30-30. If you get confused by the numbers on fertilizer bottles then don't worry, we'll cover that in a moment. But if you do get confused by them then we're better off buying a premixed fertilizer rather than purchasing the raw materials to make our own. Whatever we purchase will still be diluted in water but the package can be read and it will have instructions for you to follow.

We've already referred to these numbers as the NPK ratio, so let's dig into what that means. Plants need a bunch of nutrients and micronutrients. The macronutrients they need are nitrogen, phosphorus, potassium, calcium, magnesium, and sulfur. Also included in these are hydrogen, oxygen, and carbon. Micronutrients for them include iron, manganese, copper, zinc, boron, and molybdenum. If you are adding compost to your soil and keeping it healthy then you are going to have most of these nutrients in place in the soil. This is refreshing since trying to balance all of these would be a lot of effort. We have to primarily worry about six. Hydrogen is found in water and we provide plenty of water to our plants throughout the growing season. We make sure that the soil drains quickly and this also lets both oxygen and carbon get to the roots and so half of the necessary nutrients are provided simply by paying attention to the soil and watering your plants.

The other three important nutrients for us to worry about are nitrogen (N), phosphorus (P), and potassium (K). Together, these three nutrients play the biggest role in the development of your plant. Nitrogen is used to make the leaves of the plant grow faster and come in more fully. Phosphorus is used by the plants to strengthen the roots and make them grow big and strong. Potassium is a general nutrient which is used in multiple functions of the plant that are required for it to properly use and distribute energy from the sun and the soil. The three numbers on the soil refer to these three elements. This is the NPK ratio or the NPK balance and it tells you the percentage of nitrogen, phosphorus, and potassium in the fertilizer. It will always be in that order, NPK, so many labels don't bother labeling the numbers on the front.

Knowing what these numbers mean makes it easy to understand these fertilizers. For most plants, select a fertilizer that is balanced around 30-30-30. This will provide a spread of nutrients to the plants. However, there are some vegetables that like a lot of one particular nutrient. For example, onions really like having lots of nitrogen and so you may go with a nitrogen heavy mixture with a ratio around 50-20-20. If you research your plants prior to seeding your gardens then you can group together those with specific macronutrient needs and feed them a separate fertilizer. If you are going with a general fertilizer then you should stick with the 30-30-30, purchase whichever brand is the most attractive, and follow the instructions on the label for how much to dilute in water.

Spray or water your plants once every week or two, depending on the instructions of that particular brand. Always reduce the strength that you feed seedlings. Fertilizer should be applied directly to the soil around the plant and not all over the foliage itself. If the leaves of the plant start to curl back and show signs of nutrient damage then you will want to flush the soil and dilute your fertilizer more. For the most part, applying fertilizer becomes as easy as watering your plants but you should be mindful to take a pH reading of the soil from time to time. Your local gardening center will have plenty of soil pH test kits that you can purchase and use to make sure that the levels in your soil aren't off the charts. Too much and too little will make it impossible for your plants to properly use the nutrients in the soil and this can cause some major damage to your plants. It's always better to start a fertilizer routine at a weaker dosage and work up to the perfect level rather than overshoot it and hurt the plants.

Watering Your Raised Bed Garden

If you built your raised bed garden properly then watering it is going to be just as easy as watering any plants you grow outside. You are going to find that you need to water them a little bit more often than those in the ground but only by the slimmest of margins. Plants grown in containers have a tendency to need to be watered more often and raised bed gardens are no different. But they're much larger and this slows down the process to the point where it won't be very noticeable. However, if you haven't properly built drainage holes into your raised garden bed frame then watering is going to make for a much more complicated experience. While raised beds do offer plants better protection from issues like root rot, a poor design can wipe that protection out and leave you with rotting plants.

Building drainage holes into your raised bed frame isn't very complicated. You can use a drill to add holes or cut out a slit along the width. Whatever method you choose to use, this will open up your raised bed garden to the outside environment. We use some netting over the hole so that the water can drain but lifeforms have a much harder time getting in. This doesn't prevent critters entirely but it does reduce the frequency. One of the best features of raised bed gardens is the improved drainage. But if you create an environment in which water gets trapped in the soil then you are putting your plants in danger. It is always better to err on the side of dry rather than wet and you need to be mindful of this starting from the design of your raised bed frame itself.

Another way we avoid having water stay in our soil too long is to water our plants in the morning. One of the biggest helpers we have when it comes to keeping our plants dry is the sun. While we need water to properly drain out from the bottom of our raised garden beds, we also need the sun to evaporate water so it leaves from the top. This act of evaporation only happens when the sun is out and so watering plants at night is a terrible idea. When you do water at night, the water never leaves the soil from the top and so it can get stuck in the bed. Doing this once might not kill your plants but if you make it a habit it surely will. You should water first thing in the morning. If this isn't possible then try to water your raised beds before noon.

The question of how often you should water your plants is going to depend on what those plants are. Some only need to be watered once a week and others need to be watered twice, maybe even three times a week. There are a couple factors that will help to determine if you need to water more often or less often but there is a general rule of thumb that gives you an accurate measurement of if you should water them or not. The finger test is one of the oldest gardening techniques we have and yet it continues to be one of the most useful even after centuries. Simply take a finger and stick it an inch into the soil. If it feels moist then it isn't time to water. If it doesn't feel moist then pull your finger out and take a look at it. If there is any soil clinging to it then it is still a little moist and you should wait. If there isn't then it is time to water the plants. This technique will sometimes be performed at half an inch rather than an inch, depending on the plant being grown.

Using the finger test will tell you if it is time to water them or not. You may quickly get into a rhythm of how often you need to water your raised beds but you need to be careful not to get too confident if it is your first time gardening. The temperature is going to change throughout the growing period and this is going to affect the rate of watering. Keep applying the finger test every day during your crop so that you understand what a garden bed goes through with the seasons and as the plants mature and come to harvest. The higher the temperature, the quicker the soil is going to dry out and the more you will have to water your plants. You will also notice that full sun garden beds need to be watered much more often than full shade beds do. They have a much easier access to the evaporating rays of the sun after all.

Another element that will change how often you have to water your plants is the soil itself. We have mixed our own soil to allow for quick draining. It's not as quick draining as potting mixture for succulents would be but it drains quickly for a general purpose garden soil. So while we can trust our soil to drain quickly at first, it is going to degrade over time. The clearest sign of this will be reflected in longer drainage times. If you are being mindful of how often your plants need to be watered then you are going to be able to tell exactly when it is time to amend your soil.

Keeping Your Raised Garden Bed Healthy and Safe

We have already spoken about pests and critters in the garden but it is worth remembering that our raised beds are not immune to these problems, even if they are less likely to face them thanks to their design. It is when we stop bothering to check for warning signs that trouble seems to find us. There are a few simple steps you can follow to keep your plants safe from harm. The first and one of the biggest is simply not to over-water them. We just finished talking about it but the issue is that important. Root rot will kill a plant so quickly, it's heartbreaking. So the first safety step is to master the art of watering your raised bed gardens.

The next safety step is to add a neem oil treatment to your weekly schedule. Just like you fertilize your plants once a week, you should spray them with neem oil as often. You can get it in a sprayable bottle or mix your own by purchasing neem oil and diluting it with water. While fertilizer is applied directly to the soil, neem oil is sprayed onto the leaves of the plant itself. This is a natural substance that tastes disgusting to pests and critters but isn't harmful in the least. If you are going to be eating the plants you are growing them you need to remember to wash them off after you harvest them but this should be your first step when harvesting vegetables anyway. A neem oil treatment is useful to help fight and prevent pests like aphids and other small bugs.

While raised beds have problems with pests far less often than ground level gardens do, you should still make checking for them a part of your routine. Checking daily is the best bet. It doesn't need to be very hard or overly time-consuming anyway. Take a piece of tissue paper with you while you are out finger testing the soil to see if it is ready to water. Wipe down the bottom side of the leaves of each plant. You aren't trying to clean the plant but simply kill any small bugs that are hanging out under there. If the tissue comes back bloody then you have some unwanted guests. You may also notice bite marks in the leaves or discoloration. Fighting an infestation mostly comes down to hosing off the plants and then applying some rubbing alcohol to the infested areas but it can take forever and it may spread throughout an entire garden bed. The big question we need to ask is how did this infestation begin?

Infestation most often starts with dead plant matter. Something drops off from your plant. It is still filled with enough food to interest a pest but nobody is trying to kill it while it hangs out there. These hiding spots need to be removed on a daily basis. Making daily pest checks and daily plant matter checks might not be an option but it should be done at least as often as you water your raised garden beds. This plant matter is especially dangerous because it can introduce disease into your garden bed while it starts to rot. We want to use compost in our beds but we need to prepare it. When we just let any ol' organic matter hang out in our gardens we end up with sickness or bugs. We've tackled bugs, so let's move onto sickness.

Sickness is pretty much always a threat and it can come from anywhere. Once it gets into a raised garden bed it can easily spread between plants. So we want to make sure we have healthy plants that can resist sickness. We also want to do our best to remove pests and dead plant matter. Pests may carry sickness and spread it between plants but they also weaken our plants by eating them. We should be careful when treating our plants. If we need to trim them then we should figure out how to achieve the results we want in the least amount of cuts. Each cut is like a punch to the plant and they can only take so much of a beating at one time. The more beat up a plant is, the easier it is for disease to get in and hurt it. Same with open limbs after trimming back branches. There are creams that you can purchase to put over healing plants but it is better to simply reduce the amount of trauma as much as possible rather than treat excess trauma.

If you are cutting your plants, always clean the tools before and after. You don't know what might be left on your tools or what might have found its way there while you weren't using them. For the health of your plants, always use clean tools. This is especially important when you consider how trapped plants in a raised bed garden are. There is nowhere for them to move, their roots can't grow out to escape the confines of the bed. If disease or pests get in there then they are spreading. You need to reduce these risks by maintaining your garden.

And that just leaves us with critters. Critters can be adorable. Have you ever seen a deer eat from your raised bed garden? It's utterly adorable… for about ten seconds, then it becomes a major pain in the butt as you chase it away and assess the damage. The worst part with critters is that they are big enough to destroy a raised bed garden in a hurry. That deer you just saw? You only stared at it for ten seconds but that doesn't tell you how long it was there eating away. It might have just had a ten course meal in your garden while you were still making your morning coffee. Critters are high risk threats when it comes to gardening.

Trying to deal with the damage caused by a critter is often fruitless. They get in, eat their fill, and they leave you with either a ruined crop or a massively reduced yield which might not even be worth bringing to harvest anymore. Since critters are such destructive threats, our best bet is to prevent them rather than try to deal with them after the fact. With critters, prevention isn't spraying the plants with neem oil like you do with pests. Instead, critters need to have their access to the plants blocked. This can prove to be quite troublesome and very unattractive depending on where you built your raised garden beds. If they are in the middle of your yard without much around, then fencing may look completely out of place and really pull the observer's eye in an unappealing way. The best way to avoid this problem is to plan your critter protection while you are designing your raised garden beds. This will allow you to either work from the natural features of the land itself or to build protection into the designs for the bed itself, thus creating a sense of unity between the raised beds and the protecting fence.

Fencing is the best bet for keeping out deer. If you don't live in an area with many critters, you may think that this threat isn't a problem for you. But if you have even the smallest amount of woods near where you live, then you should prepare yourself for deer. They have been known to find gardens by following their nose like a cereal mascot. While a bigger threat in the countryside, they will wander into urban areas for a snack if they are hungry enough. Our fencing is a simple defensive addition which prevents deer from getting close enough to eat. This can be done by placing a full wooden fence around your raised garden beds, or by tightly stringing up some mesh fencing around the plants. If you go with mesh then you will probably want to attach it to the bed itself so that it is tall enough to prevent a deer from reaching their head over it. You will also want to be careful about how you attach it to the garden bed, as you still need to be able to get access to the plants to tend to them. One way to do this is to design a breakaway section from your raised bed frame. Attach your wire fence to the breakaway section, then simply remove it when you come to work on your plants. Snap it back into place when you're done and you have deer protection which you can quickly add or remove as needed.

If you are dealing with smaller critters then the wire fence will certainly help but you need to be extremely careful about how tightly it is connected to your raised garden bed. If there is a lot of space between the bottom of the fence and the raised bed frame, then this gives small critters a way into your garden bed. You need to make sure that any wiring you use is nice and snug against the frame. As you are stringing up your protection, make sure you run a finger under the bottom of the fence. Anywhere that your finger easily slips into it, you will want to tighten up either by using staples, nails, or a strong glue. If you've ever seen the kinds of tiny cracks that a cat can fit through then you have firsthand knowledge of how flexible and determined a critter might be. This is especially true when we talk about a critter that's trying to figure out how to score a bite to eat. Hunger is the mother of invention in the animal kingdom, after all.

We've already talked about the risk of pests and critters getting into our raised bed gardens from below. We know that we have to add drainage holes to our raised bed frames and so we added a layer of mesh over the bottom in order to prevent anything from getting in that way. Unfortunately, this doesn't lower the risk to zero. There will always be the risk that something may dig their way in. Typically, they'd come up against the mesh and figure that it isn't worth their time and effort to dig through. But a determined critter can easily chew through that mesh protection if they've got enough time. Unfortunately, it can be extremely difficult to identify a problem of this sort before it gets into your raised garden bed. There may be signs around your yard that point you towards a problem but this isn't very likely if you only have one or two burrowing critters in the area. They can easily go unidentified, as the signs of their passing are minimal if you can't find any holes. What this ultimately means is that burrowing critters don't really become a problem until it is too late. Thankfully, they don't eat as much as deer and you can spot an intruder early if you are mindful of your plants.

When a burrowing critter has gotten into your raised bed, you should be able to tell immediately. If you have been monitoring your plants every day, then you will have a pretty good idea of how your plants are supposed to look. Or, at least, how they looked the last time you checked in on them. A burrowing critter moves through the soil underneath your plants and so when it starts to move upwards for a feast, all of that displaced soil starts to mess with the integrity of the plants in the bed. If you wake up and find your plants leaning in odd directions or toppled over, but no sign of a deer and no trace of strong winds, then you can be pretty sure you have a burrower in your bed. You may even be able to hear them in the bed itself. If so, remove them while wearing gloves and a long sleeve shirt just to be safe. You may need to call a local animal group or exterminator to remove it from your property and check for others. Meanwhile, your garden bed will also be exposed from the bottom. If you can access the bottom of your raised bed easily, then you may be able to patch it up, but chances are you will have to wait until after the harvest in order to repair the damage. If this happens then you need to be extra mindful of your plants. They can be kept healthy and safe until harvest but warning signs of danger need to be picked up on immediately and dwelt with swiftly.

Finally, there is one more threat you need to consider, especially if you decide you want to start growing delicious fruit like strawberries or raspberries. These are super attractive to all forms of critters and so the precautions you take for deer and digging rodents most definitely need to be put into place. But you also have to worry about the sky when you are growing berries and other sugary treats. Birds love berries, as this personal story shows.

I live in an area which has lots of farmers and gardeners. A lot of my friends got jobs working in the fields but one of them scored an office job in the building next to what we all called "Blueberry Acres." As far as you could see, there were blueberry fields all around this office building. It was lovely to look at but every few minutes there would be what sounded like a cannon being fired. This was to scare off the birds, because they were the biggest threat to the harvest. During the fruiting season, all sorts of birds of all different species would descend on the blueberry field and eat as much as they could before a gunshot spooked them off. They would then fly over to the office building to paint its white walls blue and cover the parking lot in blue droppings. They are known as "blueberry bombers" and they are still a major threat to those fields to this day.

We might not be able to make so much noise in our backyards, surely the neighbours wouldn't be a fan of it. But we can protect our raised garden beds from birds by setting up netting around it. You can purchase mesh netting and string it up yourself but most garden centers sell protective covers for your individual plants. Either of these will frustrate a bird's efforts to get at your berries. This can make for an ugly looking crop, though. If your raised garden beds are close to the house then you can probably get away with simply keeping an eye on them from the window and yelling at birds that stop by. If you frustrate their efforts, they will eventually move on to find easier meals.

There are a lot of ways that our gardens can be damaged or become a snack for a cute critter. While this section could be fairly called fear mongering, it is important to know all the possible risks that we face. Most of us won't encounter all of these but many of us will encounter a few of them if we keep gardening for any length of time. It is always better to be prepared. With that said, let's talk about the most common danger you will encounter: weeds.

Tackling Weeds Before They Take Over Your Raised Bed Garden

Weeds are far less likely to get into a raised bed garden than they are one on the ground but somehow they always do. More than pests, disease, or critters, weeds are a menace that you will surely encounter even if you only stick with gardening for a single season. One of the biggest ways we reduce the presence of weeds is by using a raised bed frame with a bottom. The drainage holes will offer them one way of entry but this is multitudes smaller compared to an open bottom bed. Yet, they will get in through those drainage holes at some point. They'll also find ways to get in from the top as well. When it comes to weeds, finding a way into your garden is pretty much all they are good for. We'll briefly look at some of the worst and discuss the best method for removing them.

Weeds aren't necessarily bad in and of themselves. Some of them, like dandelions, can be quite pretty and even tasty in salads. The problem with them is the fact that they aren't wanted. Weeds like to grow and spread as quickly as can be. If you wanted a yard full of crabgrass, then you could do this easily and be satisfied. But when you want a yard full of different types of flowers, herbs, and vegetables, then crabgrass spreading everywhere isn't such a great thing. Even if you could keep the spread of a weed controlled, its roots would still be stealing nutrients away from your plants in order for the weed to grow. They are aggressive in the way they suck up and consume nutrients. Removing them when you see them is always key.

Grasses are among the worst of the worst when it comes to weeds. Already mentioned, crabgrass is pretty much one of the worst weeds to deal with. It lives all across North America and it spreads quickly, choking out garden beds in no time at all. It starts to grow in the summer and so you find yourself fighting it around the time you would be preparing to harvest and shut your beds down. If you are growing in the ground then you are going to want to carefully study the way that these harmful grasses look. But since we're growing raised bed gardens, we can go ahead and just remove any grass that starts to grow in our beds. Other harmful types include Johnson grass, which you need to place straight into a bucket or wheelbarrow when you remove or it will continue to grow; quack grass, which not only sucks up nutrients from the soil but it also releases chemicals which paralyze the plants in your bed and stunt their growth; and Bermuda grass, which is nearly unkillable and spreads faster than the plague. When growing herbs, make sure you study their appearance ahead of time so you don't mistake them for one of these grasses and yank them out. Or worse, you mistake one of these grasses for the herbs and end up with a garden bed full of Bermuda and crabgrass.

Another annoying type of weed is those which actually use the term in their names. Hearing someone mention bindweed or chickweed, you can tell pretty quickly that they're either growing cannabis wrong or they are dealing with two of the worst weeds out there. Bindwind, also known as wild morning glory or creeping Jenny, is the closest thing to a zombie we've got in the world today. This stuff just won't stay dead and even though it is a cousin of the sweet potato, there is nothing sweet about it. Then there's chickweed, which some gardeners cook up and eat or use to treat skin irritation. Yet this weed spreads out lots of seeds that can take up to a decade to germinate. That means you could yank out some chickweed next week, only to find out in 2029 that it had spread seeds throughout your raised garden bed.

Other weeds to watch out for include dandelions, ground ivy, burdock, and Canada thistle. You can kill off burdock by pouring vinegar on it but this isn't a great idea when you're tending to a raised bed garden. Burdock grows the most in soil that hasn't been worked a lot. So if you are growing your plants in rows then you will want to take a hoe to the strips between each row. If you tilled the entire bed when you were seeding then you are less likely to encounter this weed. Ground ivy is a hard to remove weed which likes to spread out across the surface of the soil, which makes it easy to spot at least. Canada thistle produces pretty pink flowers but these can cut your hands if you aren't careful to wear gloves. Finally, dandelions are the stereotypical North American weed, that one flower that seems to grow everywhere no matter how many times you remove them.

Removing weeds is one of the hardest parts of tending to any type of garden. Our raised bed gardens will deal with them less often but they are also higher risk in many ways. Since everything is self contained, weeds can wreak serious havoc if they aren't treated quickly. There are some herbicides which gardeners can use to take care of them but doing so also risks the health of your plants. It is also easy to cause damage to the soil if you aren't being careful of how much you are using and what the effects it has on the soil are. While herbicides offer the quickest route for dealing with weeds, it is hard to recommend their use. If you do plan to use a herbicide, at least stick to an organic one rather than a chemical concoction made with ingredients you can't pronounce.

The best way to remove weeds is to use your hands and a cutting tool like shears or a hoe. It is common to hear someone describe removing weeds as "pulling weeds." It is thought, with some merit, that the best way to remove a weed so that it doesn't continue to grow in your garden is to yank its roots out of the soil. It is true that this is one way to prevent the weed from returning but this risks damaging the plants you are purposefully growing. We can't see what is happening under the soil and so we don't know what the roots are doing. They could be tangled up with the roots of your plants and yanking on them could damage the plants you are trying to save. So while pulling weeds is the quickest way to battle them, it causes unnecessary casualties. Instead of pulling them, it is better to focus on their above ground parts.

When you spot one of the weeds we've discussed, or any of the local varieties you've asked about at your local gardening center, then you should get out your tools and either cut off or break off the above soil part. You will want to remove this from your garden immediately, as it is now just dead plant matter that will attract pests and disease. Don't even bother with the weed's roots. It will begin to grow back and when you spot this, remove the above soil part yet again. Do this as many times as it grows back. Eventually, the weed will give up. The roots will stop trying. Now, left over the winter, these roots can decompose and add nutrients back into the soil. This method of weed removal will require more effort, as you need to kill the same weeds several times but it won't damage your plants and it will even help to replenish your soil. That extra effort goes a long way towards maintaining your plants and your garden so that it lasts you for a lifetime.

RAISED BED GARDENING

Chapter Summary

- The most time consuming part of gardening is taking care of our raised bed gardens throughout the season and in the years to come.

- It is important to keep our soil nice and healthy. One way we do this is by mixing compost into it from time to time, either at the start of the growing season or at the end.

- There is such a thing as too many nutrients, so it is important that we don't go overboard and amend our soil too often.

- Organic components in the soil are going to break down over time. This will lead to soil which doesn't drain as quickly. You are going to want to amend it to drain faster and put more nutrients back into your garden bed.

- You should protect your garden soil before winter by either covering it with a tarp or by adding a layer of compost and then a layer of mulch.

- We can add soil fertilizers to our garden beds but the control we have with a liquid fertilizer can't be beat. Since we will be adding compost to the soil before most winters, it is better to stick to liquid fertilizer so we can avoid overfeeding.

- Fertilizers are made up of a mixture of nitrogen, phosphorus, and potassium, as well as other micronutrients that aren't used as much. These three elements make up the NPK ratio of our fertilizer. In general, stick to an NPK balanced fertilizer such as a 30-30-30 blend.

- Follow the instructions on your fertilizer to figure how much water to dilute it in and how often to feed your plants. Start with a low dose but work your way up, typically applying weekly. Apply fertilizer to the soil and not over the plants themselves.

- You should not overwater your garden bed, as this will lead to root rot. Use the finger test by sticking your finger into the soil to see if it is moist before watering. Only water dry soil. It is better to let your plants go a little dry.

- Water in the morning and never later than midday. The sun will help to evaporate water in the soil. If you water at night then there will be more moisture trapped overnight and this threatens the health of your plants.

- How often you should water your plants is going to be determined by what species you are growing. Then this will be altered depending on how much sunlight the soil gets, how warm it is, and how well the soil drains.

- You should apply neem oil to your plants weekly to protect them from pests.

- Pests are less of an issue with raised bed gardens but they will still get in. Make sure that you remove dead plant matter to help reduce the threat. Always check your plants, including the underside of their leaves where pests like to hide.

- Disease can come from anywhere but it loves dead plant matter. Be mindful to clean your raised garden beds often to remove the risk. Also be aware that plants are weaker when they are being hurt. Trimming will hurt your plants, as will being chewed on by pests, and these shocks will make them more susceptible to disease.

- Always sterilize your gardening tools after you use them to avoid spreading contamination.

- Critters are going to want to eat any fruits or vegetables you are growing in your raised garden bed. Critters that dig under the soil will be rare cases when you have a bottom as part of your raised bed frame but they could still get in. Birds are a hassle when you are growing fruit but it is deer that are the most harmful. Limit critters' access to the garden by adding fences, netting, and other protective measures.

- Weeds spread like crazy. You need to be watching your gardens closely to spot them early. When you do, don't pull them out of the soil. Their roots might be tangled up with the roots of your plants and this isn't any kind of good. Instead, break off the top part and remove it from your garden. Continue doing this whenever it grows back, eventually the roots will give up and die. As they decompose under the soil, this will bring more nutrients back into the soil.

In the next chapter you will learn how to avoid common mistakes that beginners make when starting their first raised bed gardens. These can be both time- and money-consuming and avoiding them will save you from some major headaches. Knowing is half the battle, so learn from others' mistakes so you don't lose the fight.

CHAPTER SIX

COMMON MISTAKES TO AVOID

If you have been paying attention throughout the book then a lot of what you read in this chapter will be information that you encountered before. This is because the book is written to give you all the information you need to garden like a pro. Simply put, you have already learned the right way to plan and care for a raised bed garden. When you learn the right way, you avoid making mistakes by acting on assumption and instead act with knowledge and comprehension.

With that said, it never hurts to be thorough. If you've been paying attention, then hopefully you find yourself nodding along with the understanding of how these common beginner mistakes could easily be avoided. If you haven't been paying attention then this chapter is especially for you. If you don't want to make the rookie actions that cost time, money, and energy, and cause major headaches and stomach pains then you are going to want to pay careful attention to these common mistakes that beginners keep making.

Overwatering Your Plants

This is the last chance there is to reinforce the idea that it is better for your plants to be too dry than too wet. While plants need plenty of water, too much water is the deadliest thing of all. It gets into the soil around the roots and prevents them from sucking in oxygen. The roots will blacken and die. They go from having a solid texture almost like a piece of string and instead start to feel slimy and gross. This is all happening under the soil, though, so the first sign that most gardeners see is when the leaves of their plants start to go mushy as they rot from the inside, and if you aren't regularly checking your plants you might not see it until the whole plant has started rotting. If you notice this early on the lowest leaves, you might be able to save the plant by digging it out to remove the rotted roots but more often than not it is already too late.

So the best way to avoid this tragic experience is to avoid overwatering your plants. Always give the finger test before watering and if you are unsure then be cautious and wait a day. It only takes a moment but it can save you the work of removing and replanting your crops. Plants will begin to wilt when they are overly thirsty and this can be a sign to water them. But make sure this wilting isn't just due to the noonday sun. Some plants will wilt in order to protect themselves from the hottest temperatures of the day. Once the sun starts to set, they will stop wilting. Since you should never water your plants at night anyway, check for wilt in the morning to get a more accurate reading. Noonday wilting has tricked many beginners into a panicked watering in the afternoon and this leaves water in the soil overnight. Even if your plants appear to be dehydrated, wait until the morning to water them. It may feel odd but it is the healthier option.

Skipping Out on Maintenance

Maintenance is so important that we just finished an entire chapter discussing it and we're still going to briefly touch on it again. This is another one of those mistakes that happens often enough to be embarrassing. There is simply no excuse for leaving your garden completely untended to. When you do this you are choosing to completely ignore any signs of danger that you might have been able to catch early. If you left your house for a vacation, you would lock the front door. When you stop maintaining your raised garden beds, you are basically leaving them with their door wide open for pests, weeds, critters, and disease.

The biggest problems with untended beds are weeds and dead plant matter. Weeds will completely take over a raised garden bed if you don't catch them early. Skipping out on maintenance for half a week could lead to an infestation you are unable to beat without replacing the soil. Weeds that get out of hand will starve out your plants and this will lead to far more leaves dropping off them than normal. This increases the amount of dead plant matter in the garden bed and offers more space for pests and diseases to get an entry hold. Both weeds and dead plant matter are issues on their own but when maintenance is left ignored they end up being a one-two punch to your raised garden bed and the health of your plants.

Ignoring the Drainage

When you mix up your own soil, you are doing it to create a quickly draining texture. Raised garden beds drain better due to their elevated positions but you still need to use well-draining soil. Introducing too many plants will block up the soil and slow down the draining, while preventing any one plant from getting enough nutrients. Weeds will also slow down the drainage. But the biggest problem is failing to include drainage holes in the raised bed frame itself. Depending on the material used, water will have an easier or harder time getting out even with a drainage hole. You need to balance this all when building and mixing a soil. Many beginners only take into account their soil or their drainage holes and not the whole spectrum of influence.

Using the Wrong Soil

We mixed together a general purpose garden soil mixture in chapter two. This mixture will work for many plants but not for all of them. You need to do your research on what you are going to grow to see if this soil mixture will work for them. Typically, most of what you want to grow is either going to enjoy this or it will want something with a little more of a sandy texture. More minerals in the soil will increase the speed of drainage but not every plant enjoys a sandy soil.

The disappointing thing with using the wrong soil is that you may not realize it is wrong when you first start using it because it does a decent enough job. You might think that your plants are doing fine, when they are actually smaller than they should be. But when you provide them with a soil that is right, you will notice a major difference in the size and depth of color they take. This is especially true if the soil you have chosen doesn't have enough nutrients in it.

But the other issue with soil is that what was the right soil last year might not be the right soil a year later. The quality of soil degrades over time, more so if it is reliant on organic components like compost. It is important to pay close attention to your soil. Degrading soil will start to drain much slower. You may need to mix in some more minerals and compost but this can be hard to do after you have planted your raised beds for the year. A good way to get a heads up on this issue is to water your beds before you plant anything. Doing this will let you see if they are draining properly or not. Take a few minutes to also dig through the soil and see if it "feels" right. If you have been using the same soil mixture for some time then you will have a sense of how it is supposed to feel. If it feels off then it will be time to amend it to make sure it still works as intended.

Making Your Raised Beds Too Wide

Your raised garden beds, or even those beds in the ground themselves, should never be more than four feet wide. This is done so that you can tend to all of the plants in the bed, including those in the middle that are the hardest to reach. You may believe that you can reach a little further than that and so might make a larger raised garden bed but you will find that once your plants start to come in it gets a lot harder to reach those middle ones than you expected. While they are seeds or seedlings, there is nothing obstructing your view or reach but once foliage starts to grow in it can become like trying to navigate through a miniature jungle.

Remember that length doesn't matter. You can make your beds as long as you want, it is purely about width. However, if you have blocked off one of the long sides of the raised bed by having it up against a house or barn then you will want to go with a slightly thinner design no wider than three feet. It pays to be cautious about the size and placement of your raised garden beds for more than just sunlight.

Building Raised Beds Too Close Together

This pairs well with not making your raised garden beds too wide. If you are going to be placing garden beds next to each other then you should make sure there is two feet or so between them. You might be able to get away with a foot and a half but it is better to have a little more space than not enough. The reason we don't make our raised garden beds more than four feet wide is so that we can access all of our plants in order to keep an eye on them and maintain their health. This is the exact same reason that you want to have enough space to be able to easily maneuver between your beds. If you can't properly move around the garden bed then you are effectively cutting off access to an entire side and reducing your ability to properly look after those far away plants.

This is even worse when you consider that the reason this happened is because of a second raised garden bed and this means there are twice as many plants getting neglected. You might really want to squeeze two beds into a small patch of direct sunlight but doing so might put your plants at risk and defeat the whole purpose. In a case like this where there is very limited space to fit two raised garden beds, stick with just one. Grow a few other sun-loving plants in containers that you can easily move out of the way while you tend the plants in the raised garden bed. Just remember to return the potted plant to its sunny spot after you are done. This will take a little more effort but it beats entirely neglecting a bunch of your plants.

Using the Wrong Material

Again, we've already covered the importance of using a safe material when building our raised bed frames but this needs to be stressed again. There are plenty of safe materials that you can use like concrete, stone, bricks, hardwoods, and more. But there are also materials which degrade the quality of the land and the soil. Tires might be an easy way to add some circular imagery to your landscaping but they should only be used for non-edible flowers since they could seep heavy metals into the soil. Then there are downright deadly materials like railway ties, which are so toxic to the land around them that there have been several government issued warnings against their use in the United States. It is important to make sure that the material you are using isn't going to end up taking a bite out of your or your plants' health.

Poisoning the Growing Environment

This one ties in directly with using unsafe materials. One of the reasons that raised bed gardening is so attractive is the level of control it gives gardeners over the growing environment. While the soil in your backyard might not be healthy at all, you take control of the soil you use in your raised bed garden so that you know it is perfectly safe and healthy. However, there are many ways in which careless gardeners may poison this soil or even the environment around the raised bed garden itself. One example of this would be to use railway ties, but the material used to make the raised bed frame is only one method of poisoning the environment.

Another way is to use chemical fertilizers, pesticides, fungicides, or herbicides on your garden. If you don't know what you are spraying on your plants then you won't even know if you are doing something good for them or harmful to them. One of the reasons that organic gardening has been getting so big lately is precisely because organic practices move away from using harmful chemicals. When used on a raised garden bed, the first thing that will get sick is the soil of the raised bed. Since we designed our beds to have proper drainage, chemicals will be able to drain out of the raised bed and into the soil itself. So what starts out as a contained poisoning will quickly become one that affects the land around the raised bed, too.

While we're discussing this as a beginner mistake, the sad truth is there are many "experts" who make this particular mistake all the time. In fact, many large farming empires use very unsafe practices and the chemical runoff from their plants has even ended up contaminating nearby lakes and rivers. Avoid poisoning your garden and the world around you by staying organic.

Not Preparing for Winter

Raised garden beds need to be protected for the winter. Many gardeners ignore this step, both with their raised beds or with flower beds directly in the ground. Then, come the next spring, they wonder why their soil is such low quality. This shouldn't be a surprise but it seems many beginners don't realize that they need to prepare for the winter the same way that the birds and bears do. The soil needs to be kept safe from the elements.

RAISED BED GARDENING

The easiest way to do this is to get a tarp from your local gardening center and use this over top of the raised beds. However, a more natural and rewarding way to do this is to spread a layer of compost over your soil and then a layer of mulching. This will keep your soil safe from the elements, while also letting the compost decompose and turn into nutrients to enrich the soil. Make sure that you get some protection down before the first major snow storm of the season.

Not Weeding Pathways

The bigger issue with weeds is when they infest our raised bed gardens. But we shouldn't ignore their presence in and around our raised bed gardens. When we do, we are simply inviting the inevitable to happen. We're only a strong breeze away from a seed being carried up and into the garden bed. You should always weed the pathways around and between your raised beds to reduce the presence of weeds. Reducing their presence will likewise reduce the likelihood of infestation, plus it will leave your gardens looking much nicer.

RAISED BED GARDENING

Chapter Summary

- By following the information in this book, you will avoid these beginner mistakes naturally. That said, it is important to be explicitly aware of them.

- Overwatering your plants will lead to root rot. Root rot starts in the roots and turns them black and slimy. It eventually spreads throughout the whole plant and kills it quickly. Always water in the morning, never at night, so it has more time to evaporate. It is better for plants to be too dry than too wet.

- Maintenance is the most time-consuming aspect of gardening and a lot of the time it feels like you are doing it for nothing. But skipping out on maintenance is the fastest way to invite problems into your raised bed garden. Often, once a problem gets in it is too late to do anything about it except try to limit the damage.

- Ignoring the drainage of your raised bed garden frames will result in a poor experience fraught with root rot and confusing signals from your plants. They will want to be watered but they'll also be in soil that is too moist for them.

RAISED BED GARDENING

- It is important to make sure that the soil you mix up for your plants is designed for your plants. Compost-heavy soil for plants that prefer minerals isn't going to go over well. Remember that the right soil is determined by the needs of your plants, but also that a great soil will degrade over time and need to be amended or replaced.

- Raised garden beds that are more than four feet wide will make it nearly impossible to reach plants growing in the middle. This leads to neglected plants that become risks for pests and disease. Keep your raised garden beds under four feet in width to avoid this problem.

- Also make sure that there is enough room for you to move around between your raised garden beds. When you make pathways too tight, you end up not using them very often and these results in more neglected plants. You want to always be able to reach your plants comfortably.

- Using a poor material for your raised garden bed frame will not only lead to problems in repairs but there are many materials which will poison your garden bed.

- Other ways of poisoning your growing environment include using chemical-based solutions such as pesticides, fungicides, or herbicides. These can damage the soil in your raised garden bed, as well as leak out and damage the surrounding soil. Stay organic.

- Always prepare your garden beds for winter by either using a compost/mulch layer or an insulated tarp from your local garden center.

- Remove weeds from the pathways around your raised garden beds to reduce the risk of infestation.

FINAL WORDS

So there you have it. Everything you wanted to know about getting into raised bed gardens is now in your hand. It is my hope that this book has helped to answer many of the questions you had about starting your own raised bed garden. From why you would want to start one through to how it's done and how it is maintained, my goal has been to give you the information you need to get started. But that has only been half of my goal.

Giving you the information you need to get started is important but I have tried my best to stress the importance of researching your plants and listening to your garden. Taking the time to spend a few minutes every day with your garden will let you gather in firsthand experience what you would learn from a year of studying. Reading how it is done in a book is one thing but actually getting your hands dirty and learning to listen to your plants will take time and effort. It might sound like a lot of work but once you get into a flow of things, it is easy to lose track of how much time you are spending in your garden. It becomes such a peaceful hobby.

But it is also so rewarding. Watching the way your plants grow and thrive due to the careful consideration you have taken in setting up their raised bed home is a truly magical experience. Whether you are growing for beauty, consumption, or profit, you will find that the best part of the whole project is spending time with your plants and learning how they grow and communicate with us, their environment, and each other.

I hope that this book has left you with plenty of new questions and lots of ideas for how you could create wonderful raised bed gardens of your own. Make sure you take lots of photos to share the beautiful designs you've come up with so that you can inspire others to take up raised bed gardening themselves.

www.ingramcontent.com/pod-product-compliance
Lightning Source LLC
Chambersburg PA
CBHW050322120526
44592CB00014B/2013